W9-CDW-993

FROM THE LIBRARY OF

Shirley A. Charles

# IS SEX NECESSARY?

OR

## WHY YOU FEEL THE WAY YOU DO

By

JAMES THURBER AND E. B. WHITE

*Blue Ribbon Books*
GARDEN CITY, NEW YORK

# CONTENTS

FOREWORD     xi

PREFACE     xvii

I    THE NATURE OF THE AMERICAN MALE:
A STUDY OF PEDESTALISM     1

II    HOW TO TELL LOVE FROM PASSION     34

III    A DISCUSSION OF FEMININE TYPES     55

IV    THE SEXUAL REVOLUTION: BEING A
RATHER COMPLETE SURVEY OF THE
ENTIRE SEXUAL SCENE     73

V    THE LILIES-AND-BLUEBIRD DELUSION     92

VI    WHAT SHOULD CHILDREN TELL PARENTS?     112

VII    CLAUSTROPHOBIA, OR WHAT EVERY
YOUNG WIFE SHOULD KNOW     133

VIII    FRIGIDITY IN MEN     160

ANSWERS TO HARD QUESTIONS     180

GLOSSARY     189

*"Things look pretty bad right now"*
—MAJ. GEN. BRIGGS, AT SHILOH

ANY reader who has already begun to be confused by the drawings in this book should turn to Page 195, where they are explained.

# FOREWORD

DURING the past year, two factors in our civilization have been greatly overemphasized. One is aviation, the other is sex. Looked at calmly, neither diversion is entitled to the space it has been accorded. Each has been deliberately promoted.

In the case of aviation, persons interested in the sport saw that the problem was to simplify it and make it seem safer. They introduced stabilizers and emergency landing fields. Even so, the plain fact remained that very few people were fitted for flying.

With sex, the opposite was true. Everybody was fitted for it, but there was a lack of general interest. The problem in this case was to make sex seem more complex and dangerous. This task was taken up by sociologists, analysts, gynecologists, psychologists, and authors; they approached it with a good deal of scientific knowledge and an immense zeal. They joined forces and made the whole matter of sex complicated beyond the wildest dreams of our fathers. The country became flooded with books. Sex, which had hitherto been a physical expression, became largely mental. The whole order of things changed. To prepare for marriage, young girls no longer assembled a hope chest—they read books on abnormal psychology. If they finally did marry, they found themselves with a large number of sex books on hand, but almost no pretty underwear. Most of them, luckily, never married at all—just continued to read.

It was because we observed how things were going with marriage and love that we set out, ourselves, to prepare a sex book of a different kind. In this venture we were greatly encouraged by our many friends of both sexes, most of whom never thought we could do it. Our method was the opposite of that used by other writers on sex: we saw clearly in what respect they failed, and we profited by their example. We saw, chiefly, that these writers expended their entire emotional energy in their writing and never had time for anything else. The great length of their books (some of them ran into two volumes and came in a cardboard box) testified to their absorption with the sheer business of writing. *They clearly hadn't been out much.* They had been home writing; and meanwhile what was sex doing? Not standing still, you can better believe. So we determined that our procedure would be to approach sex bravely, and frequently. "Approach the subject in a lively spirit," we told ourselves, "and the writing will take care of itself." (It is only fair to say that the writing *didn't* take care of itself; the writing was a lot of work and gave us the usual pain in the neck while we were doing it.)

At any rate we gathered about us a host of congenial people of all types, mostly girls. Gay, somber, petulant, all kinds. We also got a lot of dogs, mostly Scotch terriers, a breed noted for stoicism, bravery, and humor. Thus equipped, we set about the work with a good spirit, and by dint of a rather unusual energy were able to prepare the book for publication and see it through the press without giving up any social engagements or isolating ourselves from the sexual world. Furthermore, all the time we were writing the book, we continued to earn our living—in itself no easy matter.

We early resolved to keep alive our curiosity about things. Wherever we went we asked questions. Aware of the tangled sexual thread running through the pattern of people's lives, we continually asked the question: "Why is it that *you* never got straightened out?" The answers we got to this question helped us immeasurably.

Although most of our research was in life's laboratory, so to speak, we wish also to express our indebtedness to those authors whose writings on the subject inspired us. How can we forget, in this connection, such men as Will Durant, Samuel D. Schmalhausen, Dr. Joseph

Collins, Joseph Wood Krutch, and Gardner Murphy?

Most particularly are we desirous of acknowledging a debt to those two remarkable men, who, more than any others, gave us the courage to go on; two men without whose example we never could have found in sex a daily inspiration; those two geniuses whom it is our pleasure to call the "deans of American sex,"—Walter Tithridge and Karl Zaner.

# PREFACE

MEN and women have always sought, by one means and another, to be together rather than apart. At first they were together by the simple expedient of being unicellular, and there was no conflict. Later the cell separated, or began living apart, for reasons which are not clear even today, although there is considerable talk. Almost immediately the two halves of the original cell began experiencing a desire to unite again—usually with a half of some other cell. This urge has survived down to our time. Its commonest manifestations are marriage, divorce, neuroses, and, a little less frequently, gun-fire.

When society decided it would have to set up laws to govern these polymorphous manifestations of a once simple urge which had got out of hand, it did so without a very clear notion

of sex as we know it today. It did not realize that direction of the Love Urge by outside forces of law and order must be subversive of the complete flowering of the individual—and is there anything in life more wonderful than a completely flowered individual, man or woman?

Yet under all the weight of social regulation, the ancient desire to unite and to separate and to unite again, usually with some one else, has survived, for the simple reason that it is stronger than man-made law and because cells, as now constituted, are more astute than the police. They have to be. Thus we find men and women being consistently together even against the rigorous dictates of a prescribed behaviorism to whose institutional coldness the warmth of their emotional natures is irrevocably opposed. And so on.

As far as I can make out, the authors of this remarkable book subscribe to the modern ideal of freedom in sex, but do not believe that marriage has yet been proved a failure in every

case, nor that sex can profitably be examined entirely apart from that old institution. In this viewpoint the authors and myself are at one, which is probably the reason I was asked to write an introduction.

Marriage, as an instrument, is a well-nigh perfect thing. The trouble is that it cannot be successfully applied to the present-day emotional relationships of men and women. It could much more easily be applied to something else, possibly professional tennis. As they now stand, marriage and sex militate against each other. If marriage is to be retained it must be perfected to meet the new demands and intricacies of sex. There is, doubtless, a discoverable plane on which marriage and sex, the institutional and the emotional, could meet and, as who should say, become friends. Not only marriage, however, but sex as well, would have to make certain concessions. Tempered by this balanced viewpoint, one must find it, then, logically impossible to pose only the question, "What is wrong with marriage?" It becomes

necessary also to pose the question, "What is wrong with sex?" For if it is plausible to assume that something may be so radically wrong with a well-nigh perfect institutional device that it might be well for society to abandon it, one must, in all fairness, entertain the suspicion that something may be so wrong with a well-nigh perfect emotional relationship that it might be well for society to abandon it, too.

People never have been satisfied with marriage. If the contracting parties are satisfied with it, some one else isn't. How often one hears the expression, "I don't know what she sees in him." As a matter of fact, however, we hear that expression less frequently today than we used to, because psychology has enabled us to know what she does see in him. There is, however, still considerable doubt as to what he sees in her. Some authorities claim that no man can see all there is to see in a woman, because she is too complicated and mysterious for him. This notion—that Woman is more incompre-

hensible than Man—has persisted for centuries. It is of a piece with the legend that Woman is deserving of a certain form of idolatrous worship, a legend that grew up in the early ages of the world. When Man first came into being, he did not think that the female was extraordinary. He did not think that anything was

*Early Woman.*

extraordinary. The world was unattractive physically, and a little dull. There was no vegetation, and without vegetation there can be no fancy. Then trees came into existence. It was trees that first made Man begin to brood. In pondering their leafy intricacies he got his first crude concept of beauty. He used to tear great branches out of trees and take them home

to his cave woman. "Here," he would say to
her, "lie on these." The man then reclined in
a corner of the cave and watched the woman's
hair mingle with the leaves, and her eyes shine
through them, until he fell asleep. His dreams
were troubled. Woman came into his dreams
as a tree, then a tree came into his dreams as a
woman. He also got her eyes, shining through
the leaves, all mixed up with the moon. Out
of this curious and lamentable confusion grew
the tendency in Man's mind to identify Woman
with the phenomena of the burgeoning earth
and the mysteries of the illimitable heavens. As
time went on Man rather enjoyed cultivating
this idea. It was something to think about. It
wasn't much, but it was something. Thus was
the subconscious born, with all its strange mixture of fact and symbol.

As the vegetation of the earth grew more lux-
uriant Man grew more moody. Each new plant
represented something that he could not easily
fit into his practicable scheme of things (the to-
mato, for example, wasn't fitted in until late in

the nineteenth century). For the first wild iris, Man saw no conceivable use. However, he plucked it. It had, he noticed, that curious color, or pigmentation, which he associated with only two other things—the sky and Woman's eyes. He brooded upon this astounding coincidence overlong. Often he got wet

*Early Conference.*

through, standing in a bog, contemplating a blue flag. Then he would take it home and give it to his mate.

All these things operated to bring about in Man's mind an inclination to identify the wonders of the earth and sky with the physical fact of his mate's existence. He decided they must have a great deal in common, these wonders and this woman. What that was he determined to find out. Too proud at first, too male, to take his mate into his confidence in the matter of his uncertainties, he got to tramping the bogs and woods at night, seeking the answer. He bayed questions at the moon, he beseeched the trees to speak, he shouted at the wild iris. There was no answer. It was then that it occurred to Man that, since these things could not tell him the answer to the riddle of the universe, the only possible source of that information must repose in the living creature which he identified with them, the woman with skyey eyes and leafy hair. Then came that important night when one of the early men resolutely rose from his knees, under the moon, and started back to his cave to demand from his mate an explanation of all these mysteries. On the way a star fell. Those ages were notable for falling meteors. This one frightened the man as it crashed sizzling through the trees and buried itself with a moan

in the ground. He ran the rest of the way home, arriving breathless and white.

"Wha' was 'at?" he croaked, pointing behind him. His mate saw nothing but the waving of fern fronds in the wind, the form of some animal slinking into the woods.

"It is nothing," she said, and smiled, and ran her hand through his hair.

Right then and there Man conceived the notion that Woman was so closely associated, so inextricably entwined with the wonders and terrors of the world, that she had no fear of them. She was in quiet league with the forces of life. She was an integral part of the stars and the moon, she was one with the trees and the iris in the bog. He fell down on his knees, the pitiable idiot, and grasped her about the waist.

It is inconceivable that a myth as strong as this belief in the ineffability of Woman, as deeply rooted in the soils of time, can ever be completely eradicated. However fantastical, however untrue, crotchet or whim, fancy or foible, there it is and there it has always been. To destroy it would be to put the female properly in her place, as a plain, unadorned unit in the senseless but unending pattern of biological continuity. Romantic love would disappear. Life would be simplified. Neuroses would vanish. But Man clings to his ancient and silly value. What it has done to him is quite easy to see. It has subordinated him to Woman, for one thing. The emotional nature of the male has either been overlooked altogether or greatly disparaged. "Isn't that just like a man?" is an all-too-glib and common expression. It implies that one can virtually ascribe to all men the simple reactions which, in a number of men, inexpertly observed, have proved *likely* to take place. (The italic is mine.)

Observers have been too prone to hold that the male is negligible, and to overemphasize the importance of the female. Thus we find such keen analysts as Ira S. Wile and Mary Day

Winn [1] asserting that "anyone who wishes to understand modern marriage must center his attention on woman and find out what she thinks of it and what she intends to do about it." This is the old Bridegroom Fallacy—the notion, to paraphrase Miss Loos, that the bride is divine but that the bridegroom is just nothing. Unless more stress is laid, and pretty quickly, too, upon the complexity of the male, and the importance of what he is thinking about and what he intends to do, or at least what he would like to do, we are never going to arrive at a norm. How often do you hear it said that the little whims and desires of a man should be cherished, or even listened to? You don't hear it said at all. What you do hear is that "the way to a man's heart is through his stomach.' A thing like that hardens a man. He may eat his spinach and say nothing, but he is being hardened just the same.

The American male, because of the remarkable stress laid upon women in this country, has

[1] *Marriage in the Modern Manner.*

been understood least of all males. There has been no completely successful attempt to state his case until the authors of this extraordinary book came along. I do not know who they are. In places they do not seem to be themselves. But they've got something. (A lot of what they have they seem to have got from Zaner and Tithridge, which is all right with me.) At any rate, they state the case for the American man clearly and plausibly. At the same time they have by no means neglected the female. It takes two to make a neurosis, and nobody knows that any better than White and Thurber, unless it's Zaner and Tithridge.

Herein are examined, therefore, both men and women, male and female, Man and Woman—not only in themselves, but in their curious reactions to each other. The term "reaction" seems to be used in this book to include not only those quick, unpremeditated reflexes which cause so much trouble, but also those slowly formulated prejudices, doubts, and suspicions which cause even more trouble. If

this book does anything at all toward straight-
ening out the lamentable mess that things have
got into in America—and I certainly think it
will—the authors will feel amply repaid for
their pains, which consisted in large part, they
tell me, of insults.

LT. COL. H. E. L. LE BOUTELLIER, C.I.E.
SCHLAUGENSCHLOSS HAUS,
KING'S BYWAY,
BOISSY-LE-DOUX SUR SEINE.
*July 15, 1929*

# CHAPTER I

## THE NATURE OF THE AMERICAN MALE: A STUDY OF PEDESTALISM

IN NO other civilized nation are the biological aspects of love so distorted and transcended by emphasis upon its sacredness as they are in the United States of America. In China it's all biology. In France it's a mixture of biology and humor. In America it's half, or two-thirds, *psyche*. The Frenchman's idea, by and large, is to get the woman interested in him as a male. The American idea is to point out, first of all, the great and beautiful part which the stars, and the infinite generally, play in Man's relationship to women. The French, Dutch, Brazilians, Danes, etc., can proceed in their amours on a basis entirely divorced from the *psyche*. The Chinese give it no thought at all, and never have given it any thought. The American would be lost without the *psyche,* lost and a little scared.

As a result of all this there is more confusion about love in America than in all the other countries put together. As soon as one gets the psychical mixed up with the physical—a thing which is likely to happen quite easily in a composing-room, but which should not happen anywhere else at all—one is almost certain to get appetite mixed up with worship. This is a whole lot like trying to play golf with a basketball, and is bound to lead to maladjustments.

The phenomenon of the American male's worship of the female, which is not so pronounced now as it was, but is still pretty pronounced, is of fairly recent origin. It developed, in fact, or reached its apex, anyway, in the early years of the present century. There was nothing like it in the preceding century. Throughout the nineteenth century the American man's amatory instincts had been essentially economic. Marriage was basically a patriotic concern, the idea being to have children for the sake of the commonwealth. This was bad enough, but nevertheless it is far less dangerous to get the commonwealth mixed up with love than to get the infinite mixed up with love.

There was not a single case of nervous breakdown, or neurosis, arising from amatory troubles, in the whole cycle from 1800 to 1900, barring a slight flare-up just before the Mexican and Civil wars. This was because love and marriage and children stood for progress, and progress is—or was—a calm, routine business. "Mrs. Hopkins," a man would say to the lady of his choice (she was a widow in this case)— "Mrs. Hopkins, I am thinking, now that George [1] has been dead a year, you and I should get married and have offspring. They are about to build the Union Pacific, you know, and they will need men." Because parents can't always have men-children when they want them, this led to almost as many women as men working on the Union Pacific, which in turn led to the greater stature of women in the pres-

[1] The late George Hopkins.

[ 3 ]

ent Northwest than in any other part of the nation. But that is somewhat beside the point. The point is that men and women, husbands and wives, suitors and sweethearts, in the last century lived without much sentiment and without any psycho-physical confusion at all. They missed a certain amount of fun, but they avoided an even greater amount of pother (see Glossary). They did not worry each other with emotional didoes. There was no hint of a Pleasure-Principle. Everything was empiric, almost somatic.[1]

This direct evasion of the Love Urge on the part of Americans of the last century was the nuclear complex of the psycho-neurosis as we

[1] The word "somatic" has been left out of the glossary because of the confusion which the dictionary itself seems to be in over the meaning of the term. "Pertaining to the wall of the body" is as close as the New International comes to what we have in mind here, but it goes right on to use "parietal" as a synonym and parietal means "pertaining to order within the buildings of a college." Then again the word goes back to the old Indian, or East Indian, root *Soma* which means a god, a liquor, and an asclepiadaceous climbing shrub (*Sarcostemma acidum*). Furthermore, if your eyes stray even a fraction of an inch, in looking up "somatic," you are in "sölvsbergite" which includes the feldspars, ægirite, grorudite, and tinguaite.

know it today, and the basis for that remarkable reaction against patriotic sex which was to follow so soon after the Spanish-American war.

At the turn of the century, the nation was on a sound economic basis and men had the oppor-

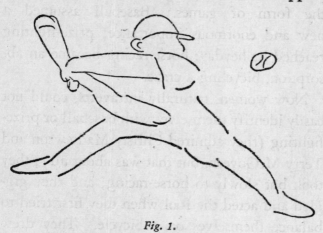

**Fig. 1.**
*Sex Substitutes (Übertragung Period): Baseball.*

tunity to direct their attention away from the mechanics of life to the pleasures of living. No race can leap lightly, however, from an economic value to an emotional value. There must be a long period of *Übertragung,* long and tedious. Men were not aware of this, thirty years ago, because the science of psychology was not far advanced, but nature came to their aid by supplying a temporary substitute for an emotional sex life, to tide them over during the period of *Übertragung*. This substitute took the form of games. Baseball assumed a new and enormous importance; prize-fighting reached its heyday; horse-racing became an absorption, bicycling a craze.

Now women, naturally intraverts, could not easily identify themselves with baseball or prize-fighting (they admired Christy Mathewson and Terry McGovern, but that was about all); they took but slowly to horse-racing; and they giggled and acted the fool when they first tried to balance themselves on a bicycle. They drew away from men and from men's concerns, there-fore—there was no more of the old Union Pacific camaraderie—and began to surround the mere fact of their biological destiny with a nimbus of ineffability. It got so that in speaking of birth and other natural phenomena, women seemed often to be discussing something else, such as the Sistine Madonna or the aurora borealis. They became mysterious to themselves and to men; they became suddenly, in their own eyes, as capable of miracle and as

*Fig. 2.*
*Sex Substitutes (Übertragung Period): Bowling.*

worthy of worship as Juno and her sisters. This could not go on. The conflict was ineluctable.

When men, wearied of games, turned to women with that urgency so notable in the American male for its simplicity and directness,

[ 7 ]

they found them unprepared for acceptance and surrender. The process of adjustment in courtship and in marriage became more involved than it had ever been before in the history of the country, if not in the history of the world. The new outdoors type of American man, with all his strength and impetuosity, was not easily to be put off. But the female, equipped with a Defense far superior in polymorphous ingenuities to the rather simple Attack of the male, was prepared. She developed and perfected the Diversion Subterfuge. Its purpose was to put Man in his place. Its first manifestation was fudge-making.

The effectiveness of fudge-making in fending off the male and impressing him with the female's divine unapproachability can not be over-estimated. Neither can its potentiality as a nuclear complex. The flitting from table to stove, the constant necessity of stirring the boiling confection, the running out-of-doors to see if the candy had cooled and hardened, served to abort any objective demonstrations at all on

### FUDGE-MAKING.

*"The female, equipped with a Defense far superior in polymorphous ingenuities to the rather simple Attack of the male, developed, and perfected, the Diversion Subterfuge. The first manifestation of this remarkable phenomenon was fudge-making."*

the part of the male. He met this situation with a strong Masculine Protest. He began to bring a box of candy with him when he called, so that there would not be any more fudge-making. These years constituted the great Lowney's era in this country. Brought back to where she had started, face to face with the male's simple desire to sit down and hold her, the female, still intent upon avoidance of the tactual, retaliated by suggesting Indoor Pastimes—one of the greatest of all Delay Mechanisms. All manner of parlor games came into being at this period, notably charades,[1] which called for the presence of other persons in the room (Numerical Protection). The American male's repugnance to charades, which is equaled, perhaps, by his repugnance to nothing else at all, goes back to those years. The Masculine Protest, in this case, was a counter-suggestion of some games of his own, in which there was a greater possibility of personal contact. His first suggestions were quite primitive, such as that it would be fun to

[1] See Glossary, definition No. (1).

[ 11 ]

count up to a hundred by kissing. The female's response was the famous one of Osculatory Justification. There must be, she decreed, more elaborate reasons for kissing than a mere exhibition of purposeless arithmetical virtuosity. Thus Post Office and Pillow were finally devised, as a sort of compromise. Neither was satisfactory to either sex. The situation became considerably strained and relationships finally trailed off into the even less satisfactory expedient of going for long rides on a tandem bicycle, which has had its serious effects upon the nature of the American man. He liked, for one thing, to do tricks on a bicycle. The contraption was new to him, and he wanted to do tricks on it. One trick that he liked especially was riding backwards. But there wasn't one woman in ten thousand, riding frontwards on the rear seat of a tandem wheel, who would permit her consort to ride backwards on the front seat. The result of all this was not adjustment, but irritability. Man became frustrated.

Frustration wrought its inevitable results.

"There wasn't one woman in
ten thousand, riding frontwards on the rear seat of a
tandem wheel, who would
permit her consort to ride
backwards on the front seat.
The result of all this was not
adjustment, but irritability.
Man became frustrated."

Men began to act jumpy and strange. They were getting nowhere at all with women. The female gradually assumed, in men's eyes, as she had in her own, the proportions of an unattainable deity, something too precious to be touched. The seed of Pedestalism was sown. The male, in a sort of divine discontent, began to draw apart by himself. This produced that separation of the physical and the psychic which causes the adult to remain in a state of suspended love, as if he were holding a bowl of goldfish and had nowhere to put it. This condition nowadays would lead directly to a neurosis, but in those days men were unable to develop a neurosis because they didn't know how. Men withdrew, therefore, quietly and morosely, to their "dens." It was the epoch of the den in America. Some marvelous ones sprang into being. Their contents were curiously significant. Deprived of possessing the female, the male worked off his Possessive Complex by collecting all manner of bibelots and bric-à-brac. The average den contained a paper-weight from

Lookout Mountain, a jagged shell from Chicka-
maugua, a piece of wood from the *Maine*, pictures of baseball-players with beards, pictures of
bicycle champions, a yellowing full-page photo-

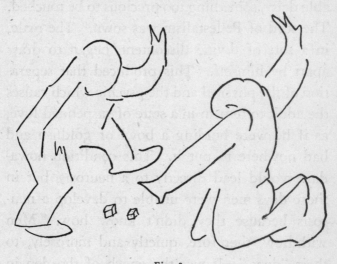

*Fig. 3.*
*Sex Substitutes (Übertragung Period): Craps.*

graph of Admiral Schley, a letter-opener from
Niagara Falls, a lithograph of Bob Fitzsimmons,
a musket-badge from the G. A. R. parade, a red
tumbler from the state fair, a photograph of
Julia Marlowe, a monk's head match-holder, a

[ 16 ]

Malay kriss, five pipe racks, a shark's tooth, a starfish, a snapshot of the owner's father's bowling team, colored pictures of Natural Bridge and Balanced Rock, a leather table runner with an Indian chief on it, and the spangled jacket of a masquerade costume, softly shedding its sequins.

The den was the beginning of male sublimation in this country, but the fruits of that sublimation were slow in ripening. At the start, in fact, they were in a state of absolute suspension. Man began to preoccupy himself with anything, no matter how trivial, which might help him to "forget," as the lay expression has it. He thought up childish diversions, at which one person can amuse himself, and to justify his absorption in these futile pastimes he exaggerated their importance, as we shall see. These diversions included the diabolo, the jig-saw puzzle, linked nails and linked keys, which men took apart and put back together again, and most important of all, pigs-in-clover.

During this period almost no achievements

of value, in art, science, or engineering, were forthcoming in the nation. Art, indeed, con· sisted chiefly of putting strange devices on boxes with the aid of a wood-burning set. The commonest device was the swastika, whose curi-

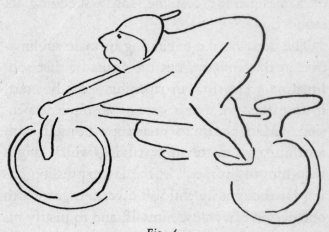

*Fig. 4.*
*Sex Substitutes (Übertragung Period) : Six-day Bicycle Racing.*

ously distorted conformation bears no discernible relationship to any known phallic symbolism. Those years were blank, idle, lost years. Outside affairs of all kinds were neglected. Men retired to their dens and were not seen for days. The panic of 1907 was a direct result. It might be interesting to examine into a typical case history of the period.

## CASE HISTORY

George Smith, aged 32, real estate operator. Unmarried, lived with mother. No precocious mother fixation. Had freed his libido without difficulty from familial objects, and was eager to marry. Had formed an attachment in 1899, at the age of 29, with a young virgin. Her Protective Reactions had been immediate and lasted over a period of three years, during which he had never even held her hand. Defense Devices: usually euchre (four-handed), or pedro. Definite and frequent fudge-making subterfuge. Post Office and Pillow, both with low degree of success.

Smith's separation between the physical and the psychic occurred in 1902, the direct stimuli presenting themselves on June 6th of that year, examination (by Dr. Matthiessen) showed. On that day Smith ran, frightened, from a barbershop in Indianapolis, where he lived. Inside the shop, on the floor, a middle-aged man named Herschel Queeper had thrown a fit. Queeper had been trying for two days to get three little balls, under a glass in a tiny round box, to roll into an opening made for them (common pigs-in-clover puzzle). But no sooner would he get the third one in than one, or perhaps both, of the others would roll out. Mrs. Queeper was beginning to wonder where he was.

Smith withdrew to his den and pondered and fiddled around and made Unconscious Drawings (Cf. Plates I, II, III and IV). He turned his attention from the object of his amorous affections to a consideration of the problems of pigs-in-clover. The usual Justification of Occupation occurred. It took the form of exaggerating the importance of finding out whether the puzzle could possibly be solved, and of working out a methodology of solving it more readily, if it could be solved at all. The case procured one of the little boxes and began to roll the balls toward the opening. At first he set about it

*UNCONSCIOUS DRAW-
ING: PLATE I.*

*Unconscious drawings, as they
are called in psychoanalytical
terminology, are made by
people when their minds are
a blank. This drawing was
made by Floyd Neumann, of
South Norwalk. It represents
the Male Ego being impor-
tuned by, but refusing to yield
to, Connecticut Beautiful.*

quite calmly. There were no immediate signs of mental deterioration, either malignant or benign. But although the case got all the balls into the opening, thus proving that it could be done, he never got them all in at the same time. In the second month he threw a brief fit. This, today, would ordinarily prove the first step toward a complete physico-psychic breakdown, but in those days neuroses were staved off longer, owing to the general ignorance of psychology, and Smith not only calmly examined the effect of the fit upon himself, without calling in any scientists, but determined to go on and examine the effects of fits upon others. He decided, however, that it would be difficult to examine the effects of puzzle-fits upon men, because men brooked no examination when they were intent upon puzzles, and so he hit on the idea of having his dog, an animal named Dewey, play with the little round box until it threw a fit. But when he called in his dog he found, after several experiments, that the dog could not hold the box in either its right or left paw.[1] Furthermore, the animal was profoundly incurious about the puzzle.[2]

Undismayed, Smith decided that somewhere in Indianapolis there must be a dog adroit

*"Furthermore, the animal was profoundly incurious about the puzzle."*

enough to handle the box and sagacious enough to grasp the idea behind it, and with a view to finding such an animal, he determined to get all the dogs in town, and all the pigs-in-clover puzzles in town, into one room and see what would happen. (Apotheosis Complex, with Plurality Fallacy.)

[1] This presented a difficulty that has not been overcome to this day.

[2] This disinterest held good up until the day of the dog's death.

Smith was able, however, to round up only about 85 per cent of the dogs of the city, because there were many who were too busy to get away at the time. Even so, 85 per cent of the dogs in Indianapolis was more than had ever been got together in one room before. The case attempted to explain the problem to the dogs in short, one-syllable talks, but the bedlam was too loud and too prolonged for him to make himself heard. Fifty or more St. Bernards and a few dozen Chesapeake spaniels listened, half-heartedly, but the others made holiday. Furthermore, eighty-four bulldogs would not permit themselves to be muzzled, and this added to Smith's difficulties. Thus, on the fifth day of the singular experiment, Smith, hearing a remarkable hullaballoo belowstairs (he worked in the attic), descended to the parlor, where he discovered the bulldogs engaged in a sort of tug-of-war, using a body Brussels carpet as a rope. (The case's mother had several days before retreated to French Lick, in a rundown condition.)

Smith grasped the carpet firmly, with some idea of wresting it away from the dogs, whereupon all of them save three began to pull against him.[1] The Exaggeration Complex under which the case was laboring gave him strength enough to meet with some small success in his first efforts to take the carpet away from the dogs. He pulled them as far as the bay window in the parlor, largely because they had not settled down seriously to winning. When they did, however, the total of three hundred and twenty-four solidly implanted feet and the virtually immeasurable tugging potentiality were too much for Smith. He was slowly pulled out into the hall, through the front door, and into the street. He stubbornly contested every inch of the way until a drug store, three blocks away, was reached. Here some one had the presence of mind to call out the fire department.

Dr. Matthiessen, who took the case at about this period in its development, attempted to re-

[1] These three had closed their eyes, to hang on, and did not see Smith.

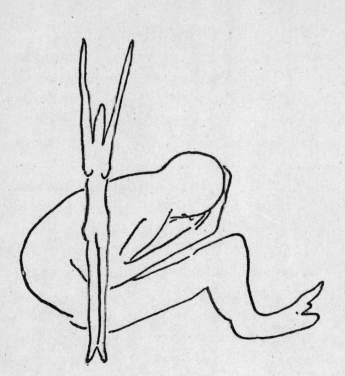

UNCONSCIOUS DRAW-
ING: PLATE II.

*This was drawn by Peter Zins-
ner, 564 DeKalb Avenue,
Brooklyn, without knowing it.
We here see Sublimation in
conflict with the Libido. Peter
has reached a point in life
where women seem so divine
he doesn't dare call them up
on the phone. Yet* **they still
call** *him.*

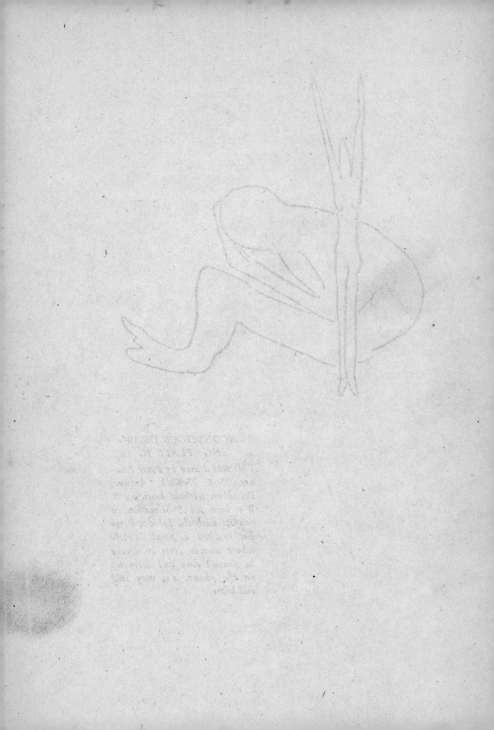

duce the Magnification of Objective, first by Analytic Reasoning, and then by cold applications. Neither was successful. Matthiessen could not divert the libido. Smith declined to resume his interest in the feminine object of his affections, and insisted that his experiment with puzzles was a glorious project for the benefit of mankind.

It was sheer accident that saved the patient— not Dr. Matthiessen. Smith finally refused Dr. Matthiessen admittance to his house, nor would he go to the doctor's office, claiming that he did not believe in psychology, but one day he dropped one of the little pigs-in-clover puzzles and broke the glass in it. He then found that he did not have to roll the balls into the openings, *but could push them in with his finger.* He got a hammer and broke the glass in all the thousands of puzzles he had brought to his home for the dogs, and solved every one of the puzzles by pushing, not rolling. This instantly released him from his complex by the Gordian Knot principle of complex release. He thus gained the necessary confidence and sense of power to feel worthy of the woman with whom he was in love, and he finally married her. The marriage was of average success.

Marriages, however, were frequently delayed much longer than in the case of George Smith, and it was not, indeed, until 1909 that the usual norm was restored. Meanwhile, in between the time of the first general separation of the physical and the psychic in this country, and the final culmination in marriages, a period of sublimation set in. This followed directly on the heels of the remarkable and lamentable era of preoccupation with trivial diversions and was characterized by an extravert interest in truly important projects and activities. The airplane was brought to a high stage of development, the telephone transmitter was perfected, tungsten replaced carbon as a filament for incandescent lamps, better books were written, art progressed, there was a cultural advance generally and the birth of a new Æsthetic, and

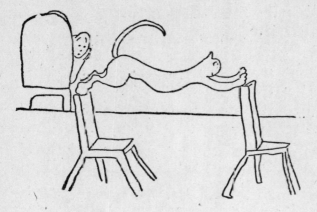

This drawing was made from an old 1901 lantern slide often used by Dr. Karl Zaner in his illustrated lecture, "What Can We Learn from Animals?" Dr. Zaner has always contended that we can learn nothing of importance from animals beyond a few pointers on the art of relaxation. "Their general activities are, as a rule, not only meaningless to man, but frequently to themselves as well. This particular cat, for example, probably had nothing special in mind at all."

people began to get at the real facts in the Thaw case. Nevertheless, Pedestalism has left its serious effects. It is doubtful if they will fully wear off for another fifty or seventy-five years.

## CHAPTER II

### How to Tell Love from Passion

AT A certain point in every person's amours, the question arises: "Am I in love, or am I merely inflamed by passion?"

It is a disturbing question. Usually it arises at some inopportune moment: at the start of a letter, in the middle of an embrace, at the end of a day in the country. If the person could supply a direct, simple, positive answer—if he could say convincingly, "I am in love," or, "This is not love, this is passion"—he would spare himself many hours of mental discomfort. Almost nobody can arrive at so simple a reply. The conclusion a man commonly arrives at, after tossing the argument about, is something after this fashion: "I am in love, all right, but just the same I don't like the way I looked at Miriam last night." Or, "Mirabel is a tidy little wench, and in that case why do I waste time composing a quatrain for her, to be sent with a crushed spray of lilac? Why don't I just go right over?"

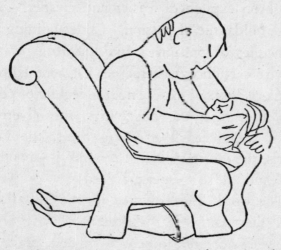

*"At a certain point in every person's amours, the question arises: 'Am I in love, or am I merely inflamed by passion?'"*

One reason a man has trouble telling love from passion is because neither term has been clearly defined. Even after one has experienced love, one finds difficulty defining it. Likewise, one may define it and then have all kinds of trouble experiencing it, because, once having defined it, one is in too pompous a frame of mind ever again to submit to its sweet illusion. By and large, love is easier to experience before it has been explained—easier and cleaner. The same holds true of passion. Understanding the principles of passion is like knowing how to drive a car; once mastered, all is smoothed out; no more does one experience the feeling of perilous adventure, the misgivings, the diverting little hesitancies, the wrong turns, the false starts, the glorious insecurity. All is smoothed out, and all, so to speak, is lost.

The word "love" is used loosely by writers, and they know it. Furthermore, the word "love" is accepted loosely by readers, and *they* know it. There are many kinds of love, but for the purposes of this article I shall confine my discussion to the usual hazy interpretation: the strange bewilderment which overtakes one person on account of another person. Thus, when I say love in this article, you will take it to mean *the pleasant confusion which we know exists.* When I say passion, I *mean* passion.

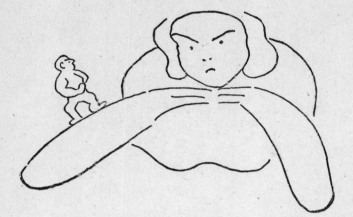

UNCONSCIOUS DRAW-
ING: PLATE III.

This is the work of Grace Mc-
Fadden, aged 11, of Bucyrus,
Ohio (R. F. D. # 3, Bucyrus
602:, Ring 3), and was drawn
on the day that Principal K.
L. Mooney, of the Paulding
County Concentration Grade
Schools, was married. Here
the Pleasure-Principle and the
Wish Motive are both over-
shadowed by the Bridegroom
Fallacy.

I have mentioned that the question of deciding whether a feeling be love or passion arises at inopportune moments, such as at the start of a letter. Let us say you have sat down to write a letter to your lady. There has been a normal amount of preparation for the ordeal, such as clearing a space on the desk (in doing which you have become momentarily interested in a little article in last month's *Scribner's* called, "Plumbing the Savage," and have stood for a minute reading the first page and deciding to let it go), and the normal amount of false alarms, such as sitting down and discovering that you have no cigarettes. (Note: if you think you can write the letter without cigarettes, it is not love, it is passion.) Finally you get settled and you write the words; "Anne darling." If you like commas, you put a comma after "darling"; if you like colons, a colon; if dashes, a dash. If you don't care *what* punctuation mark you put after "darling," the chances are you are in love —although you may just be uneducated, who knows?

Now, you have written the words "Anne dar‑ling" and have put a punctuation mark there. You pause for just a second, and in that second you are lost. "Darling?" you say to yourself. "Darling? Is she my darling, or isn't she? And if she *is* my darling, as I have so brazenly set down on this sheet of paper, what caused me to take such a long, critical look at the girl in the red-and-brown scarf this morning when I was breakfasting in the Brevoort? If I can be all aglow about a girl in a red-and-brown scarf in the early morning, is Anne my darling, or am I just kidding myself?"

Then follows a brief estimate of the compara‑tive beauty of Anne and the girl in the scarf, with the girl in the scarf coming out half a length ahead. This is followed by a short dia‑logue which you hold with yourself.

"What if she *was* prettier?" you say. "What does that amount to? I'm not a child. I know there's more to the story than mere physical beauty."

AMERICAN MALE
POSTURES: PLATE I.

American men, more than any
others, permit the complexities
of the psycho-physical world
to get them down. Often,
while down, they will pass
each other going somewhere,
and exchange a small greeting.

"What more is there?" you quietly demand, testing yourself out.

"Oh, there's quality of mind, and community of interest, and chemical attraction (chemical attraction is a term you've picked up recently from reading books on sex and life). When I get right down to it, if I were to meet that girl in the scarf, I probably wouldn't like her."

"No, but you want to meet her, all the samey, don't you?"

"Well . . . I mean . . . a man can't; I mean . . ."

"Yah, you know you want to meet her!"

"Aw, shut up!"

Having got nowhere with that theme, you again bend to the mighty task of writing the first sentence of the letter. A minute or two of quiet brooding and the truth comes to you that you have nothing to say, that you wrote all the news yesterday, that you consider it pretty silly to be writing another letter so soon, and that if anyone were to ask you, you don't really want to write Anne a letter at all.

"Well, so that's the way the wind blows!" you say to yourself, contemptuously. "So *that's* the way things are between Anne and you! Not wanting to write her. So it's come to that. Well, it's about time you got wise to yourself. If you don't love Anne it's certainly high time you found it out, in justice to both Anne and yourself. In other words, you never loved Anne at all—you merely gave in to an infatuation. You were thinking about the physical side of the affair; yes, sir, you *desired* Anne, that's what you did. You *desired* her! Why, you dirty, low-down, two-faced old voluptuary you . . ."

The utter shame of this situation breaks your spirit and you lay down your pen, light up a cigarette, and pace up and down the room. Suddenly you dash to the desk, with a look of woeful determination, seize the pen, and write (after the words "Anne darling," which are good and dry by this time): "I have been wanting to tell you something for a long time. We must look things straight in the face, Anne."

You then look things straight in the face for ten minutes, during which you don't write a word, and end by tearing the letter up and quickly dashing off another, which reads: "Anne, I'm awfully tired tonight, nervous, etc., and if I wrote you it would just be a bunch of hooey, so think I will wait till tomorrow before writing. Love, Bert." This you mail at the corner and spend the rest of the evening trying to read "Plumbing the Savage," which results finally in sleep—sleep troubled by dreams of savages wearing loin cloths of a familiar red-and-brown material.

This vexing disbelief in one's own illusion of love is experienced most alarmingly by persons of literary inclinations. Yet with them the reaction comes in quite the opposite manner. Writing is a form of sexual expression (Zaner goes further: he says writing *is* sex), and it takes just as much out of a person. Thus, a person with a bent for creative literature approaches the task of writing a love letter with an excitation of the spirit surpassing anything in the realm of pure eroticism. He anticipates it for hours, mulling over in his mind the possible material, enlarging on anecdotes, rounding off pledges of affection, sharpening similes, sharpening pencils; he comes to the writing of it with immense zeal and a rather nice control of lyrical prose; he ends on a splendidly poised and correctly balanced note of tenderness and faith and love; and then, having signed, sealed, and posted the missive, is suddenly overcome by the realization that by the very act of composition he has annulled the allure of the subject herself— cares no more about her, for the moment, than he does for an old piece of butcher's twine, which, all in all, is so alarming a discovery that he usually gets a little bit sick thinking about it, and has to go out somewhere and hear some music.

I have seldom met an individual of literary tastes or propensities in whom the writing of love was not directly attributable to the love of writing.

A person of this sort falls terribly in love,

UNCONSCIOUS DRAW-
ING: PLATE IV.

The mood captured in this
drawing is a rare one indeed,
and Dr. Karl Zaner considers
the sketch the finest in his
collection. Here the masculine
sense of Ironic Detachment
rises superior to the Love
Urge and can take it or let
it alone. The drawing was
sent to Dr. Zaner by Mrs.
Walter L. Mouse (née Kath-
leen Schaaf), recently divorced
wife of the author of the
drawing, Walter L. Mouse, of
Columbus, Ohio.

but in the end it turns out that he is more be-
mused by a sheet of white paper than a sheet
of white bed linen. He would rather leap into
print with his lady than leap into bed with her.
(This first pleases the lady and then annoys her.
She wants him to do both, and with virtually the
same impulse.)

## UNCERTAINTY IN THE MIDDLE OF AN EMBRACE

There is no more disturbing experience in the
rich gamut of life than when a young man discovers, in the midst of an embrace, that he is
taking the episode quite calmly and is taking
the kiss for what it is worth. His doubts and
fears start from this point and there is no end
to them. He doesn't know whether it's love or
passion. In fact, in the confusion of the moment he's not quite sure it isn't something else,
like forgery. He certainly doesn't see how it
can be love.

Let us examine this incident. He has been
sitting, we'll say, on a porch with his beloved.
They have been talking of this and that, with

the quiet intimacy of lovers. After a bit he takes her in his arms and kisses her—not once, but several times. It is not a new experience to him; he has had other girls, and he has had plenty of other kisses from this one. This time, however, something happens. The young man, instead of losing himself in the kiss, *finds* himself in it. What's more, the girl to him loses her identity—she becomes just anyone on whom he is imposing his masculinity. Instead of his soul being full of the ecstasy which is traditionally associated with love's expression, his soul is just fiddling around. The young man is thinking to himself:

"Say, this is pretty nice now!"

Well, that scares him. Up to this point in the affair he has been satisfied that his feeling was that of love. Now he doesn't know what to think. In all his life he has never come across a character in a book or a movie who, embracing his beloved, was heard to say, "This is pretty nice," except that character was a villain. He becomes a mass of conflicting emotions, and is so thoroughly skeptical and worried about the state of his heart that he will probably take to reading sociological books to find out if it's O.K. to go ahead, or whether, as a gentleman, it's his duty to step out before he further defames a sweet girl and soils her womanhood.

The medical profession recognizes two distinct types of men: first, the type that believes that to love a woman is not to desire her; second, the type that believes that to desire a woman is not to love her. The medical profession rests.

This young man whom I've just mentioned (the rogue who found himself having a good time in the midst of a kiss) now takes seriously to books. Matters go from bad to worse. Hoping to find, in sexology, some explanation for his conduct which would indicate that, if not decent, it at least was not without precedent, he searches relentlessly until he comes upon a chapter on "The Theory of the Libido." (Note: it makes any young man a little mad to discover that he has a *pleasure-principle,* but there it is

[ 51 ]

just the same.) On page 464 he finds this paragraph:

"The ideal healthy outcome is to find the child in whom the process of repression has been ac-

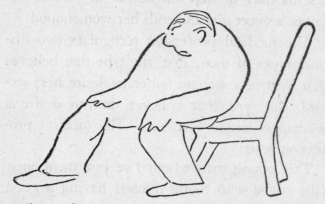

*This peculiar posture was discovered by Dr. Tithridge in a patient who for thirty years, boy and man, had been unable to tell love from passion and who allowed it to prey on his mind. Drawing from the Tithridge collection of American male postures.*

complished with no fixations of interest at lower stages of adaptation, in whom the Œdipus complex has passed into a 'normal' phase of the castration complex inhibition, and in whom a free movable libido is developing sublimation

[ 52 ]

in active interests free from paralyzing inhibitions or anti-social tendencies."

This brings the young man to the point where he thinks maybe he better lay off altogether. He just wasn't cut out for kissing, he guesses. So he writes his girl a letter apologizing for having been a beast, breaks the engagement, and goes out to Oregon, where he raises fruit fairly successfully and with no anti-social tendencies.

I have taken up the question of Man's uncertainty about love and passion in two different circumstances—at the start of a letter, and in the middle of an embrace. It was originally my intention also to show how this uncertainty overcomes one *at the end of a day in the country* when a man is so tired that he not only can't distinguish love from passion, but has all he can do to distinguish one station on the New Haven railroad from another and often gets out at 125th Street by mistake. I say this was my intention; but thus far I have been so unsuccessful in explaining the difference between love and passion that to go on would be to lay myself

[ 53 ]

open to criticism. The fact of the matter is, it's very difficult to tell love from passion. My advice to anyone who doesn't feel sure of the difference between them is either to give them both up or quit trying to split hairs.

# CHAPTER III

## A Discussion of Feminine Types

IN SPEAKING of the weaker sex in this book, the authors usually confine themselves to the generalization "Woman," "women," and "the female." For the larger discussions of sex, these comprehensive terms suffice. Yet no examination of the pitiable problem of Man and Woman would be complete without some effort to define a few of the more important types of the female. One cannot say, "Oh, well, you know how women are," and let it go at that. Many truths apply, and many foibles are common, to the whole sex, but the varieties of the female of the species are as manifold as the varieties of the flower called the cineraria.

Successfully to deal with a woman, a man must know what type she is. There have been several methods of classification, none of which

I hold thoroughly satisfactory, neither the glandular categories—the gonoid, thyroid, etc.—nor the astrological—Sagittarius, Virgo, Pisces, and so on. One must be pretty expert to tell a good

*"Successfully to deal with a woman, a man must know what type she is."*

gonoid when he sees one. Personally, I know but very little about them, nor if I had a vast knowledge would I know what to do with it. It is even more difficult, and just as unimportant, to arrive at a zodiacal classification, because that is altogether dependent upon determining the year the woman was born, and because, even if you should ascertain her date of birth, the pish-tosh of analysis and prediction which derives therefrom is a lot of mediæval guesswork. Or so it seems to me, and to Zaner, Blifil, Gorley, Peschkar, Rittenhouse, and Matthiessen.

Of much greater importance is a classification of females by actions. It comes out finally, the nature of a woman, in what she does—her little bag of tricks, as one might say.

A type of which one hears a great deal but which has never been very ably or scientifically analyzed, for the guidance of men, is the Quiet Type. How often one hears the warning, "Look out for the Quiet Type." Let us see if we should look out for it, and why.

The element of menace in the Quiet Type is commonly considered very great. Yet if one asks a man who professes knowledge of the type, why one should look out for it, one gets but a vague answer. "Just look out, that's all," he usually says. When I began my researches I was, in spite of myself, somewhat inhibited by an involuntary subscription to this legendary fear. I found it difficult to fight off a baseless alarm in the presence of a lady of subdued manner. Believing, however, that the best defense is an offense, I determined to carry the war, as it were, into the enemy's country. The first Quiet Type, or Q.T., that I isolated was a young woman whom I encountered at a Sunday tea party. She sat a little apart from the rest of the group in a great glazed chintz, I believe it was, chair. Her hands rested quietly on the chair arms. She kept her chin rather down than up, and had a way of lifting her gaze slowly, without disturbing the set of her chin. She moved but twice, once to put by a cup of tea and once to push back a stray lock from her forehead. I stole glances at her from time to time, trying to make them appear ingenuous and friendly rather than bold or suggestive, an achievement rendered somewhat troublesome by an unfortunate involuntary winking of the left eyelid to which I am unhappily subject.

I noted that her eyes, which were brown, had a demure light in them. She was dressed simply and was quite pretty. She spoke but once or twice, and then only when spoken to. In a chance shifting of the guests to an adjacent room to examine, I believe, some water colors, I was left quite alone with her. Steeling myself for an ordeal to which I am unused—or was at the time—I moved directly to her side and grasped her hand. "Hallo, baby! Some fun—hah?" I said—a method of attack which I had devised in advance. She was obviously shocked, and instantly rose from her chair and followed the others into the next room. I never saw her again, nor have I been invited to that little home since. Now for some conclusions.

Patently, this particular Q.T., probably due to an individual variation, was not immediately dangerous in the sense that she would seize an opportunity, such as I offered her, to break up the home of, or at least commit some indiscretion with, a man who was obviously—I believe I may say—a dependable family man with the average offhand attractions. Dr. White has criticized my methodology in this particular case, a criticism which I may say now, in all good humor, since the danger is past, once threatened to interpose insuperable obstacles, of a temperamental nature, in the way of this collaboration. It was his feeling that I might just as well have removed one of the type's shoes as approach her the way I did. I cannot hold with him there. Neither, I am gratified to say, can Zaner, but in fairness to White it is only just to add that Tithridge can.

However, the next Q.T. that I encountered I placed under observation more gradually. I used to see her riding on a Fifth Avenue bus, always at a certain hour. I took to riding on this bus also, and discreetly managed to sit next her on several occasions. She eventually noticed that I appeared to be cultivating her and eyed me quite candidly, with a look I could not at once decipher. I could now, but at that time I couldn't. I resolved to put the matter to her quite frankly, to tell her, in fine, that I was studying her type and that I wished to place her under closer observation. Therefore, one evening, I doffed my hat and began.

"Madam," I said, "I would greatly appreciate making a leisurely examination of you, at

*The Quiet Type.*

your convenience." She struck me with the palm of her open hand, got up from her seat, and descended at the next even-numbered street—Thirty-sixth, I believe it was.

I may as well admit here and now that personally I enjoyed at no time any great success with Q.T's. I think one may go as far as to say that any scientific examination of the Quiet Type, as such, is out of the question. I know of no psychologist who has ever got one alone long enough to get anywhere. (Tithridge has averred that he began too late in life; Zaner that he does not concur in the major premise.) The Quiet Type is not amenable to the advances of scientific men when the advances are of a scientific nature, and also when they are of any other nature. Indeed, it is one of the unfortunate handicaps to psychological experimentation that many types of women do not lend themselves readily to purposeful study. As one woman said to me, "It all seems so mapped out, kind of."

I am a little reluctant to report one other adventure with the Quiet Type, and that is why I seem to have summed up in the preceding paragraph without mentioning it. However, I now feel that some brief outline of the case I have alluded to should be set down here—espe cially after all this allusion. This young lady was a guest at a week-end party where I was also a guest. On Saturday evening it began to appear, quite early, that there was going to be considerable drinking. And, to be sure, there was. Among those who became, as the fellow said, a little bit uncertain of themselves, were the young Q.T. and myself. It was, in all truth, largely her fault that I reached a state of abandon from which, at her further solicitation, it was but an easy step to a feeling of sheer devil-may-care. This condition, it is perhaps unnecessary to say, militates against that fine precision of mind so essential to the best results in any scientific investigation.

I do not remember all that ensued one-half so clearly as I should like to. I have often thought deeply on the matter, striving to reconstruct the complete scene, as it were, but my efforts have been hampered by the lamentable fact that I found dwelling upon the more easily remembered scenes so delightful that I simply dwelt on them. I remember, for example, that

I was at the piano, or more exactly, on it—standing on it.  The Quiet Type, fearing that I might fall, grasped me firmly about the knees, and I did fall.  I was not only uninjured, but I

*I asked her how I had reached the cliff—if I had walked there.  "Partly," she said.*

got to my feet laughing.  At this she began to laugh.  I had lost my glasses in the fall, and began hunting for them.  In bending over, however, I was assailed by a slight touch of vertigo, which runs in my family, and fell again.

The next that I remember is sitting on the edge of a cliff, or *falaise,* as the French call it, looking out over a lake. The young lady was beside me. "Well," she said, "what shall we do next?" I asked her how I had reached the cliff —if I had walked there. "Partly," she said. This set me to thinking. "I have lost my glasses," I said, and began hunting for them again. She again seized me by the knees, and I fell. In falling, both of us became enormously involved. I instantly arose and was about to step into the lake, when she grasped me around the waist. We both sat down. "You have gone as far as you can," she said, and tittered. "I should like to go a little farther," said I. She arose. "You're a funny man," she said, and laughed again. I grasped her, much to my surprise, by one ankle, and she began to topple toward the lake. I fell heavily backward, pulling her with me, and this doubtless saved her life. "You must be more careful," I told her. We sat up. "Don't you think you better take me home?" she said, in a singular voice—low and

[ 65 ]

odd. "Rather," I responded, and arose. I took her back to the house, which was some half-mile distant, we joined the others, and that is all I remember.

I shall always regret, of course, that I did not have full possession of my faculties during the walk to the cliff's edge, for there might have been, in the ten or fifteen minutes it must have taken, an excellent opportunity to "get at" the young woman. There is nothing quite so provocative of pleasant, revelatory talk as a quiet walk with some one at night. However, the episode ended as I have said, and a golden opportunity was lost.

In my very failures I made, I believe, certain significant findings in regard to the Quiet Type. It is not dangerous to men, but to a particular man. Apparently it lies in wait for some one individual and gets him. Being got by this special type, or even being laid in wait for, would seem to me in some cases not without its pleasurable compensations. Wherein, exactly, the menace lies, I have no means of knowing.

I have my moments when I think I see what it is, but I have other moments when I think I don't.

The Buttonhole-twister Type is much easier to come at. A girl of this persuasion works quite openly. She has the curious habit of insinuat-

*The Buttonhole-twister Type.*

ing a finger, usually the little finger of the right hand, unless she be left-handed, into the lapel buttonhole of a gentleman, and twisting it. Usually, she picks out a man who is taller than herself and usually she gets him quite publicly, in parks, on street corners, and the like. Often, while twisting, she will place the toe of her right

[ 67 ]

shoe on the ground, with the heel elevated, and will swing the heel slowly through an arc of about thirty or thirty-five degrees, back and forth. This manifestation is generally accompanied by a wistful, far-away look on the woman's face, and she but rarely gazes straight at the man. She invariably goes in for negative statements during the course of her small writhings, such as "It is not," "I am not," "I don't believe you do," and the like. This type is demonstrative in her affections and never lies in wait with any subtlety. She is likely to be restless and discontented with the married state, largely because she will want to go somewhere that her husband does not want to go, or will not believe he has been to the places that he says he just came from. It is well to avoid this type.

A charming but altogether dangerous type is the "Don't, dear" Type. By assuming a middle of the road, this way and that way, attitude toward a gentleman's advances, she will at once allure and repulse him. The man will thus be twice allured. He calls on her, and they sit in the porch swing, let us say. When he slips his arm around her, she will say in a low tone, "Don't, dear." No matter what he does, she will say, "Don't, dear." This type is a home-

*I am told that one type has actually been known to get the man of her choice down and sit, as it were, side-saddle of him.*

maker. Unless the man wants a home made for him within a very short time, it is better for him to observe the "don't" rather than the "dear," and depart. The type is common in the Middle

West, particularly in university towns, or was some few years ago, at any rate. Any effort to classify modern university types would be difficult and confusing. They change from year to year, and vary with the region. I am told that one type has actually been known to get the man of her choice down and sit, as it were, side-saddle of him. I would not give even this brief mention, in passing, to college types of the female, were they not important because they so frequently divert a man from his career and tie him down before he has a chance to begin working, or even to say anything.

The rest of the types of American women, such as the Outdoors, the Clinging Vine, and so on and so on, are too generally known to need any special comment here. If a man does not know one when he sees it, or cannot tell one from another, of these more common types, there is little that can be done for him. No man should contemplate marriage, or even mingle with women, unless he has a certain measure of intuition about these more obvious types. For example, if a man could not tell instantly that a woman was the sort that would keep him playing tennis, or riding horseback, all afternoon, and then expect him to ride back and forth all night on the ferry, no amount of description of the Outdoors Type would be of any avail.

There is, however, one phenomenal modern type, a product of these strange post-war years, which will bear a brief analysis. This is the type represented by the girl who gets right down to a discussion of sex on the occasion of her first meeting with a man, but then goes on to betray a great deal of alarm and aversion to the married state. This is the "I-can't-go-through-with-it" Type. Many American virgins fall within this classification. Likewise it contains women who have had some strange and bitter experience about which they do a great deal of hinting but which they never clearly explain. If involved with, or even merely presented to, a woman of this type, no man in his right mind will do anything except reach for his hat.

[ 71 ]

Science does not know what is the matter with these women, or whether anything is the matter. A lot of reasons have been advanced for girls acting in this incredible, dismayed manner—eleven reasons in all, I believe—but no one really knows very much about it. It may be their mothers' teaching, it may have been some early childhood experience, such as getting caught under a gate, or suffering a severe jolting up by being let fall when a boy jumped off the other end of a teeter-totter, or it may simply be a whim. We do not know. One thing is sure, they are never the Quiet Type. They talk your arm off.

## CHAPTER IV

THE SEXUAL REVOLUTION: BEING A RATHER COM-
PLETE SURVEY OF THE ENTIRE SEXUAL SCENE

THE sexual revolution began with Man's
discovery that he was not attractive to
Woman, as such. The lion had his mane, the
peacock his gorgeous plumage, but Man found
himself in a three-button sack suit. His masculine appearance not only failed to excite
Woman, but in many cases it only served to
bore her. The result was that Man found it
necessary to develop attractive personal traits to
offset his dull appearance. He learned to say
funny things. He learned to smoke, and blow
smoke rings. He learned to earn money. This
would have been a solution to his difficulty, but
in the course of making himself attractive to
Woman by developing himself mentally, he in-

advertently became so intelligent an animal that he saw how comical the whole situation was.

Thus, at the very start of the sexual revolution, Man faced one very definite problem: in becoming mentally "aware," he had become intellectually critical, and had discovered that it was increasingly difficult to make up his mind whether he really desired any one woman, however capable he was of getting her. It was the heyday of monogamy, and in order to contemplate marriage, it was necessary for a man to decide on One Particular Woman. This he found next to impossible, for the reason that he had unconsciously set up so many mental barriers and hazards.

Let me mention a few.

(1) The fear that his fiancee might get fat inside of a few years. To any mentally alert man, this thought was a strong deterrent. Quite often the man met the girl's parents. He would quickly size up her mother and make a mental calculation as to how long it would be before the daughter was in the same boat. Somehow,

*"The lion had his mane . . .
but man found himself in a
three-button sack suit."*

it took the bloom off the romance. If he was not fortunate enough to meet the parents of the young lady, he was quite apt to note things about her own conformation that seemed prophetic. A slight thickness in the neck, a trace of rotundity in the bosom, a touch too much ankle. In these portents he found much discomfort, and was quite likely to call the engagement off.

(2) The use of a word, phrase, or punctuation mark by his fiancée that annoyed him. In these early days of the sex awakening, it was not at all uncommon to find examples of the girl's using some slight phrase which had a grating effect. It was often the case that the man was literarily inclined—because literary inclinations were early found to be advantageous in sex, almost as advantageous, in fact, as the peacock's tail—and if this was the case the man was doubly sensitive to the curious little crudities, niceties, whimsies, and circumlocutions which women were afflicted with. I am thinking at the moment of the case of a young man who, in his

junior year in college, had found the girl he believed ideal for him to marry, and then one day learned, quite by accident, that she was in the habit of using the word "Howdy" as a form of salutation. He did not like "Howdy," although he did not know why. Days and nights he spent trying to reconcile himself to the idea of it, weighing the young lady's extreme beauty and affability against her one flaw. In the end he decided he could not stomach it, and broke the troth.

(3) Difference in height. If a man fell in love with a woman taller than himself (which sometimes happened), he became morose from dwelling on the objections to such an alliance. This particular situation usually had a way of settling itself automatically: there were so many reasons, real or imaginary, why the man felt that the marriage was impossible, that just the mere business of thinking about them broke him in health and he died, leaving a margin of several weeks before the date of the wedding.

(4) The suspicion that if he waited twenty-

*"He would quickly size up the mother and make a mental cal-culation as to how long it would be before the daughter was in the same boat."*

four hours, or possibly less, he would likely find
a lady even more ideally suited to his taste than
his fiancée. Every man entertained such a suspicion. Entertained it royally. He was greatly
strengthened in his belief by the fact that he

*Male Type (eastern seaboard). Definitely interested in, but
uncertain what to do about, the Female. To men of this type
many aspects of the Sexual Revolution never became clear
at all.*

kept catching a fleeting glimpse of this imaginary person—in restaurants, in stores, in trains.
To deny the possibility of her existence would
be, he felt, to do a grave injustice to her, to himself, and to his fiancée. Man's unflinching de-

sire to give himself and everybody else a square deal was the cause of much of his disturbance. Man had become, you see, a thinking being. He had come to know enough about permutations and combinations to realize that with millions of Caucasian females to choose from, the chances of his choosing the ideal mate were almost zero.

So matters went. Man, we have seen, had begun to develop himself so that he would be attractive to Woman, and in doing so had made Woman of doubtful attraction to *him*. He had become independent. He had become critical. He had become scared. Sex was awakening and it was all Man could do to keep from laughing.

Woman, on her part, saw dimly what was going on in the world. She saw it through the sweet haze of Dream. She caught glimpses of it in the mirror of her Narcissistic soul.[1] Woman was at the crossroads. She had many ways open to her, but she chose one: *she chose*

[1] This is the first mention in this article of Narcissism. You'll hear more about it, don't worry.

*to imitate Man.* At a time when sex was in transition, she had the bad judgment to begin a career of independence for herself, in direct imitation of her well-meaning mate. She took up smoking. She began to earn money (not much, but some). She drank. She subordinated domesticity to individuality—of which she had very little. She attained to a certain independence, a cringing independence, a wistful, half-regretful state. Men and women both became slightly regretful: men regretted that they had no purple tail to begin with, women that they had ever been fools enough to go to work. Women now "understood life," but life had been so much more agreeable in its original mystery.

And now we come to Sex.[1] Woman, observing that her mate went out of his way to make himself entertaining, rightly surmised that sex had something to do with it. From that she logically concluded that sex was recreational rather than procreational. (The small, hardy

[1] Are you glad?

band of girls who failed to get this point were responsible for the popularity of women's field hockey in this country, 1911-1921.) As though in a vision, the "right to be sexual" came to women. They fell to with a will. For thousands of years they had been content merely to be amiable, and now they were going to be sexual. The transition from amiability to sexuality was revolutionary.[1] It presented a terrific problem to Woman, because in acquiring and assuming the habits that tended to give her an equality with Man, she discovered that she necessarily became a good deal *like* Man. The more she got like him, the less he saw in her. (Or so he liked to think, anyway.) Just as soon as she began to put her own sex on an even basis, she found that he lost interest. Her essential Narcissism (pleasure of looking in a mirror) was met by his Begonia-ism (concept of the potted plant). Things got so that Woman spent *all* her time admiring herself in mirrors, and Man, discouraged, devoted himself quietly

[1] Zaner claims it was also amusing.

to raising begonias, which are fairly easy to raise. Sex atrophied.

But, as I say, sex was in the transition stage. Woman soon began to outgrow her Narcissism and was satisfied to snatch quick glances of herself in make-shift mirrors, such as the backs of

*"Sex atrophied."*

watches, the shiny fenders of automobiles, plate-glass windows, subway weighing machines, and such. Convinced that sex was not sin, she set out joyously to study it. How hard she studied has recently been apparent, even to persons who read only a few books a year.

New York became the capital of the sexual

[ 85 ]

revolution. It was conveniently located, had a magnificent harbor,[1] a high mortality rate, and some of the queerest-shaped apartments to be found anywhere. There are apartments in New York in which one must step across an open bathtub in going from the kitchen to the bedroom; any unusual layout like that arouses sexual desire and brings people pouring into New York from other cities. New York became the Mecca for young ladies from the South and from the Middle West whose minds were not quite made up about sexual freedom, but who thought that if they could once get to New York and into an irregular apartment, the answer might come to them.

Their mothers were against it.

"Now what can you get in New York that you can't get right here at home?" their mothers said.

"Concerts, new plays, and the opera," the daughters invariably replied. There has never, to my knowledge, been a case of a young lady

[1] New York has one of the finest harbors in the world.

telling her mother that she wanted to go to New York because she was seeking an outlet for her erotic eagerness. It was always concerts that she wanted. Often it turned out to be concerts that she got.

When she arrived in New York and secured her unfurnished apartment (usually in West Fourth Street), her mental elation was so great and her activity in making parchment lamp shades so unabating that for the first couple of weeks she let sex go. Women are notoriously apt to get off the track; no man ever was diverted from the gratification of his desires by a parchment lamp shade. At any rate, the young lady was so tired at night she could hardly keep her eyes open, much less her mind. Furthermore, she was beginning to have *Schmalhausen* trouble. *Schmalhausen* trouble is a common ailment among girls in their twenties. It usually attacks girls who have taken a small apartment *(schmalhausen)* and are reading the behaviorism essays of Samuel D. Schmalhausen. The effect of sitting within narrow walls and

[ 87 ]

absorbing a wide viewpoint breaks down their health. The pain that they suffer during this period is caused by their discovery of the lyrical duality, or two-sidedness, of life—a discovery that unbalances all sensitive young ladies in

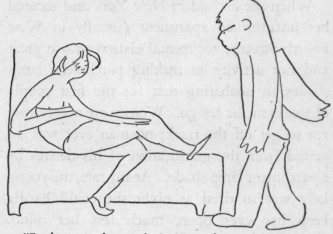

*"Furthermore, she was beginning to have Schmaulhausen trouble."*

whom sex cries for expression. Even in a New York apartment there are two sides to every-thing, and this particularly applies to a girl's potential sexuality.[1]

[1] Girls with a bad case of Schmalhausen sometimes saw as many as three sides to sex.

Let me explain this duality.

The very fact that the young lady had settled in the vicinity of Sheridan Square indicates that there was a strong vein of poetry in her. She saw life (and sex) through a lyrical haze which tended to accentuate its beauty by softening its truths. The whole purpose and scheme of poetry is to heighten the tenderness and essential goodness of life by a musical elaboration of its traditional worth.[1] Well, when the young lady allowed the lyrical possibilities of love to work on her mind, it made her mad to remember how candid she had been the night before in discussing contraception with the commercial artist who lived downstairs. It grew to be a big question in her own mind, just what her emancipation ought to consist of: whether it meant having lemon skins and gin stoppers in the wash-basin and talking freely of exhibitionism and voyeurism, or whether it meant being the recipient of some overwhelmingly beautiful passion which her poetical soul still pre-

[1] See Tithridge's "Poetry," but don't read it.

scribed but which she knew couldn't exist because she was so widely read. To stall for time
she would make another lamp shade.

Days slipped by. Always there was conflict
in her soul. She had plunged into the "candor régime" whole-heartedly; she could enter
a roomful of people and say almost anything at
all. She also went in for nudity—another outlet for sex eagerness. She dallied in the bath,
lay around the apartment without any clothes
on, appeared scantily clad at her door when the
laundryman called to collect, and week-ends
went swimming naked in the moonlight with
other young people. (Incidentally, when she
saw what a man looked like without any
clothes on, the old *Schmalhausen* trouble came
back stronger than ever.)

By and by, because of this very uncertainty
of soul, a kind of orderliness of habit crept into
her life. Unable to decide whether sex was the
poem she half believed it to be or the casual
episode she had schooled herself to think it was,
she compromised by practically giving sex the

air. She now held a good job and was earning well. Candor and nudity, with an occasional bit of exhibitionism, began to satisfy her completely. She was growing older. The apartment was nicely decorated now and teeming with lamp shades. She held some good industrial stocks and had developed an ambition to write. She became content to be literary rather than sexual. She became, in other words, that most dangerous of all by-products of the Sexual Revolution—a biologico-cultural type. She had a way of leading young men on into exhilarating topics, and sitting with them in provocative attitudes, and then putting on her hat and going quietly home to bed. In short, New York was now home to this girl, this biologico-cultural lady, and she was in a fair way to step placidly into a good old-fashioned marriage when the right man came along.

And he usually did, the poor yap.

## CHAPTER V

### THE LILIES-AND-BLUEBIRD DELUSION

THE young bridegroom who unexpectedly discovers that his wife has been brought up in extreme unawareness of the true facts of life and believes in some variant of the Birds and Flowers Delusion (that is, that birds and flowers have something to do with the emotional life of persons), is faced with a situation calling for the greatest tact and tenderness. It won't do any good for him to get mad, or to indulge in self-pity, crying, "Oh, how sorry I am for me!" and only a coward would go directly into a psycho-neurosis without first trying to win his wife over to acceptance of things as they are.

I have in mind the case of a young lady whose silly mother had taught her to believe that she would have a little son, three years old,

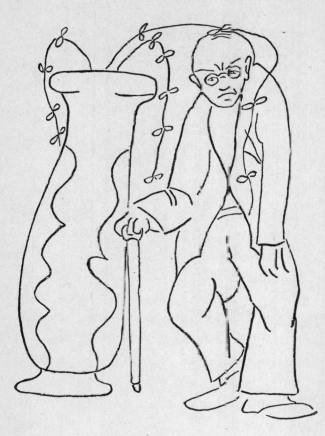

DR. WALTER TITHRIDGE
(after the etching by Veer-
bluergen).

named Ronald, as soon as her husband brought a pair of bluebirds into a room filled with lilies-of-the-valley. The young woman (to say nothing of the young man) was thus made the victim of one of the extremest cases of Birds and Flowers Fixation which has ever come to my attention. I shall transcribe, from Dr. Tithridge's notes, the first dialogue on the subject that took place between the young couple. This dialogue was carefully reconstructed by Tithridge from the account of the incident as given by the young husband, who sought his advice and counsel.

On the evening of the 25th of June, when the couple were married, the young husband entered their hotel suite to find it literally a garden of lilies-of-the-valley. He was profoundly touched, but baffled, and asked his wife who was dead.

"Where are the bluebirds?" she replied, coyly.

"What bluebirds?" he demanded.

"*The* bluebirds," she said, blushing.

[ 95 ]

Unfortunately, but not unnaturally, the bridegroom did not know what the bride was talking about. What was of the extremest importance to her, was to her husband merely an idle whim, a shadowy fancy. Obviously, the young couple should have talked such matters over long before, but they hadn't, and there they were. He strove to change the subject, whistled, lighted cigarettes, for he was nervous enough the way it was, but she kept recurring to the bluebirds. His bewilderment became tinged with some alarm, for during their courtship he had put forth no great effort to examine into her mental capacity, and he was now assailed by the excusable suspicion that she was perhaps not exactly bright. He talked rapidly, apprehensively, of many things. Among the things he talked about were the St. Louis Cardinals (a baseball club). From there it was but an easy associative step for his wife to go back to the bluebirds again.

"Aren't you going to *get* any bluebirds?" she persisted.

"I don't know where the hell I'd get any bluebirds tonight," he said, rather irritably, "me not being Bo-Peep."

The nuclear complex was made right then and there. There was a long tense silence, after which the bride burst into bitter tears.

"Now, dear," said her husband, more reasonably, "let's try to get this thing straightened out. What are you talking about, anyway?"

"Sex—if you want to know!" she blurted out, and swooned.

Instead of getting her a glass of water, he excitedly phoned the room clerk, but became embarrassed once he had got him, and merely asked that a couple of blankets be sent up. It was, unfortunately, as I have said, June—and warmish. Thus when the wife revived sufficiently to become aware of her surroundings, the husband was standing above her holding a pair of blankets, and looking pale and warm.

"What are those for?" she demanded, suspiciously, for the notion had now formed in her own mind (Dr. Tithridge feels, and I agree) that she very likely had married a dementia præcox case. These mutual suspicions of mental inadequacy are common during the first year of any marriage, but rarely are they aggravated by factors so clearly calculated to upset the men-

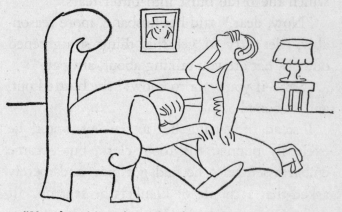

*"Mutual suspicions of mental inadequacy are common during the first year of any marriage."*

tal equilibrium as bluebirds at midnight and blankets in June. This husband and wife were drifting farther and farther apart. The solution to their problem was becoming more and more remote, what with this setting up of involved artificial barriers, this almost fantastical beclouding of the issue. Dr. Tithridge tells me that he believes the young man's reason would have been permanently dethroned had he (Dr. Tithridge) tweeted or chirped like a bird[1] on the occasion of the husband's first visit to him.

When the wife beheld her husband standing there with the blankets, she demanded, again, "What are you doing with those blankets?"

"I get cold," he mumbled, and he proceeded to put the blankets on the shelf of a closet which already held several extra pair. He was, furthermore, decidedly warm, and kept patting his brow with a handkerchief.

"Let's go out and take a walk," suggested his wife, apprehensively. To this her husband very readily agreed. They were getting afraid to stay in the same room with each other, than which there is no other condition in the world more certain to break up a marriage. Out in

[1] Experiments of this sort, calculated to determine the possible effects of tweeting, or chirping, in the case of a Birds Fixation, fall, of course, outside the province of the psycho-analyst, and not only is the legality of their practice questionable, but the value of the results obtained is highly doubtful.

the street, among people, they both felt safer, and they wandered to a bench in a fairly crowded park, and sat down.

"Where did you get the idea that birds have anything to do with us?" demanded the bridegroom.

"My mumsy," [1] she said.

"Well," he said, "she deceived you."

"About what?"

"About what you're talking about."

"Sex?" she asked.

"That isn't sex, honey," he told her. "Birds and flowers are simply . . . they do not . . . that is, we could live all our life without them."

"I couldn't," she said, and, after a pause, "I always feared *you* didn't want children."

"I do want children. I want you. You want me. Everything is going to be all right."

"How is it?" she demanded.

---

[1] Young women who allude to their mothers as "mumsy" almost invariably present difficult problems in adjustment. The word is a sentimentalization of the more common "mamma" and indicates a greater dependence upon maternal direction and supervision than may be expected in the case of young women who use the more familiar term.

"In the first place," he began, pulling at his collar, "it's this way. Now here's the way it is. Now you take me . . . or take you, say. In the first place the girl, that is Woman . . . why, Woman [1] . . ." He lapsed into a profound silence.

"Well, go on," she prompted.

"Well," he said, "you know how women are, don't you?"

"Yes," she said, doubtfully.

"That's fine," he said, brightening, "Now women are that way, then ——"

"What way?" she asked.

"Why, the way you are . . . from me . . . than I am, I mean." He made a vague gesture.

"I don't see what you mean," she said. Her husband gave a light laugh.

"Hell's bells, it's simple enough," he cried, suddenly, giving the light laugh again; "it's certainly simple enough. Now, here. We'll take

[1] Explanations of natural phenomena in terms of the collective noun, particularly where the noun becomes capitalized in the mind of the person striving to explain, are almost never successful.

Adam and Eve. There they were, all alone, see?"

"There were two bluebirds," said his wife.

"Not till after the flood, there weren't," he corrected her. "Well, he found out that there were certain essential differences—what you might call on purpose. I mean there must have been some reason. You can count on it that things like that just don't happen. Well, then, he simply figured it out—figured out the reason."

"For what?"

"For all this discrepancy. Obviously it just didn't happen. It couldn't just have happened. It had to make some sense—nature is like that. So he—so he finally—ah—what he did was tell her, see? I mean he asked her."

"Asked her what?"

"He simply asked her," said her husband in calm, almost cold tones,—"he simply asked her why she thought this was. Is there anything wrong in that? And so gradually they understood why it was. It's as simple as that!" He looked at her triumphantly.

"What *are* you talking about?" she demanded.

"Listen," he said at last, firmly. "Both of us speak a little French, and we might try it that way. I think I could explain better in French. Why, even little children, tiny girls, sing *Auprès de ma blonde* in France, and think nothing of it. It's just a nice, wholesome idea —*auprès de ma blonde*—and it sounds like poetry—but take it in English and what do you get?"

" 'Quite close to my blonde' . . ." answered his wife.

" . . . '*Qu'il fait bon dormir,*' " her husband hurried on.

" 'How good it is to sleep,' " she translated.

"Fine! Now you're talking."

"Go on," she said, "*you're* talking."

"Well, all right, but first I wanted you to see that there is no reason to get embarrassed, because everything is lovely in French. So don't mind my frankness."

"I don't," said the bride.

"All right," he began again, "*Alors,* now, *il y a quelque chose que vous avez que je n'en ai pas, n'est-ce pas?*"

"*Oui,*" she said.

"*Bon,*" he said. "*Alors, ça c'est naturel—ah —ça c'est bien naturel . . .*"

"*Par exemple,*" put in his wife, a little illogically.

"*Dites,*" he said, and after a great pause, "*Dites donc—dites vous——*"

"You should really use 'tu' and 'toi' and not 'vous,' " said his wife; "it's more intimate."

"All right," he responded. "Now, *tu as quelque chose, tu as . . . toi.*"

"*Comment?*" she demanded.

"I just don't know enough words," said the bridegroom, wretchedly. The bride put her hand on his arm.

"Let's try 'thee' and 'thou' in English," she suggested.

DR. KARL ZANER.

"That's not a bad idea," he said. "Well, all right. Now thee has ——"

"Hath," she corrected.

"Thee hath certain—ah ——"

"Differences," she supplied. "But isn't it 'thou hath'—or is it 'thee hath'?"

"To hell with it!" cried her husband. "In all thy life hast never been around, for Pete's sake?"

"Certainly, and thou—and you have no right to talk to me like that!"

"I'm *sorry*," said the young man. *"I'm* sorry." He rose to his feet. "Ye gods! to think this had to happen to me! Ah, well. Listen. I tell you what, I'll write it out for you. How about that? And if you don't like the idea, why, all right, I suppose."

It was the next day that the young husband, who had sat up all night in the hotel lobby, thinking and writing, visited Dr. Tithridge. I am happy to report that, as not infrequently happens in such cases, a solution was finally arrived at. However, in a great number of cases

[ 107 ]

the difficulty is never overcome. The home becomes a curious sort of hybrid, with overtones of the botanical garden and the aviary. The husband grows morose and snappish, the wife cross and pettish. Very often she takes up lacrosse and he goes in for raising rabbits. If allowed to go on, the situation can become so involved and intricate that not all the analysts from the time of Joan of Arc down could unravel it.

The problem is by no means any simpler where the wife is cognizant of things as they are and the husband is ignorant. I know of one young man who every night tenderly placed, with much strange clucking, a basket near the hearth into which he had some expectation that a baby would be deposited by a stork. (Plate I.) Another young husband constructed at considerable expense a water-lily pond in his back yard and fondly rowed about in it, twilight after twilight, searching for infants, laying his finger to his lip, making "tchk, tchk" noises at his wife, who watched him in profound amazement.

EMOTIONAL CHARADES.
PLATE I.

*"One young man every night
tenderly placed, with much
strange clucking, a basket
near the hearth into which
he had some expectation that
a baby would be deposited by
a stork."*

In both these cases the wives were fine women of strong character, with a background of sturdy pioneer stock, and they soon put a stop to such charades, once they divined the curiously entangled Wish Motives behind them. It may be said, indeed, that young wives are more candid and direct in their explanations of natural phenomena than young husbands, when they have to be.

The existence of such deplorable ignorance is a sad commentary on the sentimentality of a nation which sets itself up to be frankly sexual. There is much reason to be hopeful, however. The future parents of the land will doubtless come straight to the point in matters of this sort, when talking with their children. The children of today will be the parents of tomorrow, and you know how the children of today are.

# CHAPTER VI

### WHAT SHOULD CHILDREN TELL PARENTS?

SO MANY children have come to me and said, "What shall I tell my parents about sex?" My answer is always the same: "Tell them the truth. If the subject is approached in a tactful way, it should be no more embarrassing to teach a parent about sex than to teach him about personal pronouns. And it should be less discouraging."

In discussing sex enlightenment for parents, first of all, definitions are needed. What do we mean by "parents"? Do we mean all adults who have had children? Do we mean adults who have had children, they knew not why? Or do we mean married people who have given birth to one or more offspring but have never gone into the matter very thoroughly? For the purposes of this article, it will be assumed that by "parents" we mean all adult persons permeated with a strong sense of indecency.

I have talked with hundreds of children about the problem of educating their parents along sex lines. So many of them have told me that they honestly tried to give their elders the benefit of their rich experience in life, but that the parents usually grew flushed and red and would reply, "Nice people don't talk about such things." It is true that a great gap exists between generations. The fact that children are embarrassed to have their parents along when they are attending certain movies or plays is indicative of how hard it is to overcome the old fear of allowing one's elders to learn anything. A child never knows at what point in a play his uninformed old father will start to giggle. It is hard for children to break through and really come in touch with their elders. "Nice people don't talk about such things!" is the defense which old people put up against life itself, when they feel it crowding in all around their heads. Parents hesitate to discuss things calmly and intelligently with their children for two reasons: first, they have a kind of dread of learning something they don't want to know; and second, they feel that if they must learn anything at all they would like to be spared the humiliation of learning it from their offspring. Actually, middle age (and even senescence) is marked by a great curiosity about life. There is a feeling that life is slipping away quickly, and that it would be terrible to have the end come before everything in life has been revealed. The beauty of life, always apparent, implies a mystery which is disturbing right up to the bitter end. The spectacle of old men wistfully attending sex lectures (as they frequently do) suggests that the strong suspicion exists in them that somewhere they will hear the magic word by which human affairs will become clarified, somewhere they will glimpse the ultimate ecstasy. Children who allow their fathers and mothers, to whom they owe their very existence, to go on wondering about sex, are derelicts to duty.

If young folks lack the tact or intelligence

requisite to enlightening their parents, the task should be intrusted to some one else. Yet it is hard to say to whom. A child should think twice before sending his father around to public

*"One's father and mother are never too old to be told facts."*

school to secure sex information from his teacher. Women teachers, to borrow a phrase, are apt to be "emotionally illiterate." Many teachers have had no sex life and are just waiting for somebody like your father to show up.

One's father and mother are never too old to be told facts. Indeed, it is most unkind to keep them in ignorance and allow them to nourish the doubts and horrors of their imagination. The majority of parents pick up their knowledge of the facts of life from smoking-car conversations, bridge-club teas, and after-dinner speakers. They receive it from their vicious adult companions who are only slightly less ignorant than they are and who give them a hopelessly garbled version. They pick it up, too, from the gutter.

This matter of picking up information from the gutter is an interesting topic in itself. Quite the most remarkable case history that has come to my notice is that of François Delamater, a parent thirty years of age, who went deliberately to the gutter for his sex education. He had heard, as all people do hear some time or other, that sex can be learned from the gutter, so he set out to make a comprehensive survey of the gutters of eighteen large American cities. For a long time he found out nothing, although he

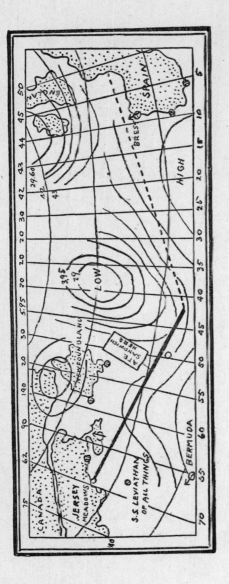

Fig. 7. It is customary to illustrate sexology chapters with a cross section of the human body. The authors have chosen to substitute in its place a chart of the North Atlantic, showing airplane routes. The authors realize that this will be of no help to the sex novice, but neither is a cross section of the human body.

was a very curious man. By a peculiar piece of fortune, however, he happened to be walking in Cincinnati one day and met a man who was leading a tame stork. The man was in the gutter. The stork carried in its bill a live baby, in swaddling clothes. Smelling a rat, Mr. Delamater stopped the man and inquired where the baby came from. The man replied that he didn't know.

"For that matter," continued Mr. Delamater, "where does *any* baby come from?"

The man shook his head. Then he relented and told Mr. Delamater that he had merely been hired to lead the stork around the streets to advertise a moving picture called "Her Husband's First-born." The whole incident so confused the mind of the thirty-year-old parent that he eventually evolved the strange theory that babies are born within the father, an erroneous notion that dwarfed his emotions and modified his character.

It is of the utmost importance, in imparting sex knowledge to one's parents that it be done in such a way as not to engender fear or anxiety. The phraseology should be chosen carefully, and efforts should be made to explain everything clearly but without the use of words which have a tendency to make old people nervous. The word "erotic" is such a word. When it is necessary to speak of Man's erotic tendencies, it is best to substitute another word. In the first place, an overwhelming majority of parents do not know the exact meaning of the word "erotic," and to know an *in*exact meaning is worse than nothing. Many are apt to confuse it vaguely with "exotic." I have known parents to go through whole books by authors like Havelock Ellis or Mary Ware Dennett without understanding a single paragraph, because they thought Man's "eroticism" referred to his desire to be in some foreign place like Spain. Those parents that actually do detect the difference between the sound of the two words will immediately become nervous, inattentive, and dispirited. They will make some excuse to leave the room, and will wander out, probably to the ice-box to get themselves a cold snack, which they will eat while in a sulky frame of mind. Later they will look up the word in the dictionary, but will forget it by the time they hear it again in conversation or read it in print. Furthermore, all their taste for sex will be gone.

Just what to tell parents is, of course, a vital question, not to be answered dogmatically. Before a child can conscientiously approach such subjects as pedestalism, the recessive knee, begonia-ism, frigidity in men, birth control, sublimation, and the swastika fixation, he must clear the boards. The simple phases of sex should be imparted in a direct manner: it is best to explain things in a matter-of-fact way, rather than resort to such cloudy analogies as birds and flowers. Strange to say, the habits of birds and flowers have done as little to clarify the human scene as almost any other two manifestations in nature. Further, there is always the danger, in setting up plant or animal life as an example, that one's parents will place a literal interpretation on things. I am thinking particularly of the case—which all sociological students know about—of Nina Sembrich, the fifteen-year-old high-school girl who attempted to impart knowledge to her father by telling him about bees. (Nina's mother was dead, or she would have told her too.) She traced, in rather minute detail, the renascence of earth in spring, the blossoming of the trees, the activity of the bees and their function in distributing the pollen, the fertilization of the seed and its growth during the warm languorous summer days, finally the fruition and harvest.

It was a beautiful story, redolent of orchards and sunny hillsides, instinct with life—a story that had a soporific effect on Mr. Sembrich, lulling him as the buzz of a bee lulls one in hot daisy fields. The upshot of it was that he gathered a rather strange impression from the narrative and somehow got the idea that to have babies you had to keep bees. He bought several hives, installing them in the little sitting-room on the second floor, where Mrs. Sembrich had kept her sewing-machine when she was

"Strange to say, the habits of
birds and flowers have done
as little to clarify the human
scene as almost any other two
manifestations in nature."

alive. The acquisition of the apiary further complicated matters for Mr. Sembrich by reason of the fact that bees themselves enjoy a rather extraordinary sexual scheme—theirs is a complex society, infinitely more diverting and harder to understand than our own. Observed by a slightly nervous person who is trying to profit by a simple analogy—as Mr. Sembrich was—bees are capable of causing the utmost confusion.

If you will recall what you know about bees, you will readily understand what I mean. In a colony of bees, certain individuals have no sex whatsoever; these are the "workers." The male bees are "drones." The queen (or "mother") bee develops her sexual character only after being arbitrarily chosen for the purpose, walled up, and fattened on special food. Mr. Sembrich marveled at these things.

Basing his hopes entirely on what he had seen, he made his first overt act, which was to give up his business (he was a merchant tailor) on the assumption that to be endowed with masculine characteristics one had to be a drone. In this, of course, he was justified to some degree; for it is quite true that very busy men rarely are fully equipped for a complete or happy sex life. Business men commonly find a vicarious gratification for their erotic nature in card index systems. Often, their satiable appetite for life is dissipated in the process of dictating a single sales letter. Only men who devote virtually their entire attention to love ever glimpse its full glory or experience its bewildering intensity. (And *they* make so little money they might just as well not.)

Mr. Sembrich, therefore, was not without justification in becoming a drone, since life was what he wanted to find out about. But it was when he undertook to fatten up a lady of his acquaintance into a "mother" that he ran into difficulties. He locked her in the kitchen and plied her with rich desserts. He even urged honey on her—a rather literal expedient even for a man in his mental condition. The lady not only failed to become a mother, but she took sick and died, surrounded by a group of Mr. Sembrich's "workers," whom he had hired to help feed her. With a dead woman in the kitchen and a lot of bees upstairs in the sitting-room, the household became unbearable as a place to live and bring up his daughter Nina, so Mr. Sembrich fled, still ignorant of the essential knowledge of life.[1]

Another case, not exactly paralleling the Sembrich affair, is the case of two parents who failed to learn something to their advantage because they happened to be at dinner. It happened this way. Charles Updegraff had sent his son, Junior, to spend the summer at a boys' camp. There, in addition to learning how to swim, paddle, and make fires, Junior learned about sex, so that he returned home fine and brown and a credit to the Updegraffs. (The Updegraffs had swum, paddled, made fires, and so on, for generations.) Now, at Camp Whortleberry (that was the name of the camp) the authorities had adopted what is known as the

[1] Sexually speaking.

"pet method" for imparting sex knowledge to the boys. Each boy was given charge of a pet of some kind, and the pets were given *carte blanche*. Junior Updegraff drew a pair of sunfish. To augment the actual pet study, the boys were also given lectures by the camp director, who knew in a general way what he was talk-

Sun fish (Mola-Mola)

ing about. Thus, when the summer was over the boys' minds were full of a strange assortment of facts and oddments, some of them rather amusing. Young Junior had hardly been home an hour when he thought he would do his old man a good turn by telling him what he knew about sunfish. The Updegraffs were at table.

"Pop," he said, "do you want the low down on a sunfish?"

Mrs. Updegraff hastily interrupted. "Better wait till after dinner, son," she said.

*"Young Junior had hardly been home an hour when he thought he would do his old man a good turn by telling him what he knew about sunfish."*

(Note: parents have always been held back by the superstitious idea that it is wrong to learn anything while eating.)

"What's the matter with right now?" asked

Junior. "I was just going to tell Pop about our pet study course. I know a lot of things."

"Wait till we're through eating," said Mrs. Updegraff.

"Why should I? A mouse is an embryo twenty days, a lop-sided apple is that way because it's been fertilized only on one side, male

Sea Rover

animals grow bright colored in the mating season, and so it goes. Sunfish . . ."

"Junior!" said Mrs. Updegraff, sharply. "Not till after dinner. Sunfish can wait!"

"No they can't!" cried Junior, warming up to his subject. "The father sunfish makes the nest, then . . ."

"We don't want to hear about it," snapped Junior's mother. "Tell us about your canoe trips."

"I never went on no canoe trips."

"Why not?"

"Always was watching the sunfish."

The matter was dropped and the meal continued in silence. After dinner Mr. Updegraff, secretly very much interested, hung around in the hope that his son would again open up the subject of sunfish. The boy never did. He was only a child and children are easily discouraged.

I suspect that the church is responsible, in large measure, for the ideas of life now held by adults. Sex is still sin to the evangelical clergy. A kiss is thinkable only when sanctified by the church. A child who permits his parents to continue in the belief that the elevation of the soul depends on the renunciation of the flesh, is hardly doing his duty by them. Sometimes it may be advisable to quote to your parents from standard works on the subject of sex. Great care must be taken, though, to avoid

[ 131 ]

abruptness, as far as possible. Thus there is some doubt in my mind whether a child ought to approach its mother on a hot afternoon when she is tired and bedraggled, and say to her: "Ma, under favorable conditions a husband and wife should remain sexually attractive to each other during the whole period of their sexual potency."

That's no way for a child to talk.

Some children have told me that instead of quoting from books they have tried leaving the books lying around, opened at pertinent pages. Even this failed to work in most cases. The mothers usually just picked up the book, dusted it, closed it, and fitted it neatly in some nearby shelf. They thought it was dusty.

Sea robin

# CHAPTER VII

## CLAUSTROPHOBIA, OR WHAT EVERY YOUNG WIFE SHOULD KNOW

THERE is an erroneous impression current nowadays that sex is everything. It is similar to the psychological delusion common during the war years that the war would never end. Man is inclined to exaggerate the immensity of his chief preoccupation. Thus when the World War was in progress, men convinced themselves that there would never be anything else but war. Then the war ended, and Man was left, as it were, stranded. Used to a tremendous preoccupation, he had to have another. He turned to sex, out of sheer momentum, and overestimated its importance as he had magnified the immensity of war.

Sex is by no means everything. It varies, as a matter of fact, from only as high as 78 per cent of everything to as low as 3.10 per cent. The norm, in a sane, healthy person, should be between 18 and 24 per cent. In these hectic days, however, it is not unusual to hear even intelligent persons say, or imply, that sex is everything. This, of course, leads to the mistaken idea that a couple who are, so to speak, emotionally compatible, are going to be compatible in every other way. "Take care of sex, and the details will look after themselves," is the rule, in a manner of speaking. Nothing could be more stupid. A man and woman may be very, very happy emotionally and not get anywhere at all. There are many reasons for this, but none is more important than the inability of many a husband, otherwise normal, to become adjusted to a lack of freedom. Freedom is as essential and as primary an urge with a man as the loss of it is with a woman. A man grows up with the desire to be free and unfettered. The boy of six wants to play outside the house all the time. He doesn't even want to come into the house for his meals. On the other hand, little girls like to be in the house as much as they can. When dusk falls, the little boys are restless under the urge to be several blocks away, playing Go, Sheepy, Go, but the little girls want to be home putting their dolls to bed. Usually at least one of the dolls is ill and needs constant attention. Often it is necessary to force little girls to go outside and get some air and exer-(cise, just as it is frequently necessary to use force to get little boys *into* the house. And even when girls do go outdoors, they have to be watched like a hawk or they will be playing house in the dog box or under the cellar door.

And yet, in spite of all this, women marry men without giving the serious chasm between their essential natures a thought. They think that a man wants a home. Well, he does, in a vague sort of way. Not so much a home, however, as a house. He likes to be able to say where he lives when he goes to vote, and things like that. But he doesn't want a home in the sense that a woman does, to potter around in. He has neither the same urge nor the same talent for hanging pictures and re-arranging furniture. A woman, no matter how opposed she may become to housework, still gets a small thrill out of shifting things. It never wears off. She may be too tired to cook and insist on going out to dinner, but before she goes she would be willing, nay, glad, to put the Victrola where the davenport is and move the davenport over in front of the fireplace. One simple move like that is enough to alarm a man sufficiently to serve as the onset of a seri-ous psychological or mental disturbance. Men don't stop to reason about individual moves. As soon as a woman calls on her husband to help her change the position of a couple of pieces of furniture, he instantly thinks the house is going to be torn up, as it was last spring, with carpets rolled up in the hall, and step-ladders and buckets everywhere. This gives him a strange "boxed-in" feeling. If that feel-ing recurs too often, the husband may get claustrophobia. Claustrophobia is "a dread of being in an enclosed space, of living under conditions which would interfere with a speedy escape into the open."

Every young wife should know the first symptoms of claustrophobia, because, if taken in time, it can be cured, but if allowed to run on, deterioration sets in and may result in anything from benign stupor to complete paranoia. Once a husband gets into the outer rim of the paranoid and paranoic psychoses, he may easily run through all of them, and in the end simply be no good at all. The first symptoms are usually innocuous enough, and may consist of nothing more than a mere Amplification of Personality Without Signs of Conflict. (The symptoms listed herein are largely selected from Claudé's table.) But from there it is an easy step up to and including Logical Development of Delusions upon False Premises, Fragmentation of Personality, Dissimulation of Egocentricity, Looseness of Systematization, Exaggerated Feelings of Prejudice, Polymorphic Delusions, Ingenious Methods of Defense, Reticence, Recourse to Legal Measures, Apathy, Writing

Letters to the Newspapers, and, finally, Diminu-
tion, or Total Loss, of Neuro-Vegetative Reflexes. There is nothing sadder than the spectacle of a once strong, firm-minded man no
longer master of his neuro-vegetative reflexes,
to say nothing of a hitherto well-integrated fellow in the throes of Fragmentation.

## AVOIDING THIS SAD STATE

There are various simple ways to avoid this
sad state of affairs. Of course, where a husband
and wife have plenty of money to begin with,
and servants take care of all the details of household management, there is very little danger of
claustrophobia. (There is always danger, even
with money and servants, of dual personality,
melancholia, and automatic writing, but not of
claustrophobia.) In wealthy marriages, which
are usually made for either financial or social
reasons, the husband and wife see little, if anything, of each other, and the husband need have
no fear of being boxed in at all. He is free to
come and go at any time. But I am dealing with

the typical American marriage, in which the wife runs her own home—builds it up around her husband—either because she has to, or because she wants to. A woman's desire to potter about her own home goes back a long way, so far back that the urge often remains when economic necessity no longer exists. Women like to do their own work. They even build up ingenious excuses for doing it, such as claiming that the maid or the hancy man didn't do it right. This desire may not last for longer than the first three or four weeks of marriage, but that is ample time for the onset of claustrophobia. During that period a wife will concentrate on buying kitchen ware, painting chairs, selecting silver patterns, building bookshelves, etc., to the complete exclusion of everything else in life. The young husband, hearing all this tinkling and rattling and shoving going on around him, smelling paint, listening to hammering, etc., will begin at once to have a fear of being trapped or "caught.' He will strive to get out of the house, and his wife should allow him to go. What she almost invariably does, however, is to stop him and ask him to hold a piece of chintz or toile de jouy up over the mantel so that she can see whether she likes it there. She won't like it there, and he then has to hold it, first high, then low, then in between, over a table in another part of the room. When this point is settled, he will likely be asked to hang a few pictures. Now a curious thing happens to many sensitive husbands when they are hanging pictures or holding things against walls. They get the impression that the walls are being made thicker, for the purpose of making it harder for them to get out—interfering with a speedy escape into the open. This is usually the beginning of the most dangerous of all hallucinations in claustrophobia cases—the Persecution Complex. The husband feels that he is not only being boxed in, but persecuted. If deterioration is allowed to set in, the delusion of persecution may attain astounding proportions, such as that the Masons or the Piano-makers are against him, or that former Vice-

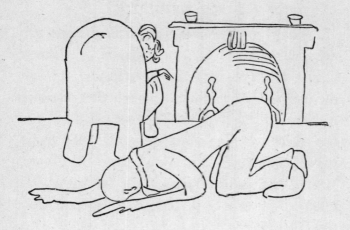

"He will strive to get out of
the house, and his wife should
allow him to go."

president Charles G. Dawes is trying to "get" him. A case history will show how this happens.

Case No. 22. *Personal History.* Normal birth and development. Born June 14, 1894. Had the usual childhood diseases with no sequelæ. No serious accidents or operations. Patient began school at the age of six, got along very well, graduating from high school at 18. Graduated from college at 22, and became an architect. He always held good positions with good salaries. Considered capable and efficient. Habits normal. Everything normal. Case married when he was 29.

*General Make-up.* Always considered keen, intelligent, amiable, and trusting. Liked outdoor activities, something of an athlete, with a strong urge to "get away by himself." Began to be suspicious shortly after his marriage. He frequently showed this suspicion in his work by complaining to his associates that his ability was not recognized, and intimating that he thought the elevators in the building had purposely quit stopping for him, so that he could not get out. Nervous. Jumpy.

*Mental Examination.* Patient was very keen, alert, but suspicious when brought under observation. His demeanor was self-assertive, but he was inclined to be anxious and restless. He demanded his immediate freedom of the physicians who were examining him, and was greatly frightened. "Let's get out of here!" he kept repeating to the doctors. He was allowed to depart, commitment to an institution not being thought necessary on the occasion of this first examination. Later the patient became violent. Would jump up from dinner table and cry, "Let's get out of this!"

*Causation.* When examined for causation, the patient at first talked guardedly, and then incoherently. "Look out for the water!" he would say, and, again, "You can't get out that way!" His physicians, unable to correlate his statements and his apprehensions, called in Dr. Damon Prill, the eminent New York psychoanalyst. "What have we here?" said Dr. Prill.

"Patient," explained one of the doctors. "Look out for the water!" cried the patient. "Where did the water come from?" asked Dr. Prill, quietly. "From the drip-pan under the refrigerator," said the patient. "Ah yes," said Dr. Prill. "You can't get out that way!" cried

*Onset of the boxed-in feeling.*

the case. "Now, why is it that we can't get out that way?" asked Dr. Prill. "Because we are painted in," said the patient. "Painted in, eh?" asked Dr. Prill. "You heard me," said the patient. "Painted in, hammered in, pictured in, davenported in"—here he made a strange

twisting gesture with both hands, leaned forward, and ended, in a confidential whisper—
"rolled up in a rug!"

The reiteration of these incoherencies was all that Prill could get out of the patient, but it was enough to persuade him to question the man's wife. He made some interesting discoveries. It turned out that the wife, one day, had asked her husband to keep his eye on the pan under the refrigerator and see that the water did not overflow, while she went to a bridge tea. The husband was home, going over some important plans. He forgot the pan and the place was flooded. The ceiling in the apartment below fell. The woman in the apartment below went all to pieces. The patient's wife, returning from her tea, went all to pieces. The patient went all to pieces. Thus the hallucination formulated in his mind that being married and living in a house necessitated going to pieces. As for being "rolled up in a rug," that, it transpired, had actually happened to him also. One day, during a thorough cleaning of the house, which his wife was superintending, she ordered two burly men to roll up a rug, without noticing that her husband was on it at the time. He was accordingly rolled up in it and had considerable difficulty getting out. As for being "painted in," Prill established that the husband was also actually painted in on one occasion. He was in the bathroom shaving, and his wife did not know it. Thus she had a man paint the floors outside the bathroom, and when the husband opened the door to emerge, he couldn't get out without stepping on the paint. He was about to step on the paint, anyway, when his wife saw him. "Here, here!" she said, "you can't get out that way!" There was no other way out. "You'll simply have to stay in there till the paint dries," his wife told him, and he did.

Prill explained to the wife what these inhibitions had done to her husband and that his condition was precarious. He stressed the importance of allowing her husband his freedom at all times, paint or no paint. The husband was then brought back into the home and was allowed to live a free, unfettered existence, coming and going as he pleased—always, however, under the discreet surveillance of Dr. Prill. With that perspicacity of psycho-mental cases, however, that almost second sight, the patient became aware that some one was snooping around, watching him, and one night he leaped out of bed, pulled open the door of a little-used closet, and there was Dr. Prill watching. The patient, who otherwise might have been cured, went instantly into the last stages of the Persecution Complex.[1]

The husband-patient began with the idea that he was being persecuted by the Detective Bureau of the Police Department and gradually enlarged his Apprehension Field until he believed he was also being persecuted by the Navy, the towns of Indianapolis and St. Louis, and the Box Manufacturers' Association. He whispered

[1] This discovery of Dr. Prill in the closet is one of the few blots on the splendid record of psycho-analysis, and is most unfortunate.

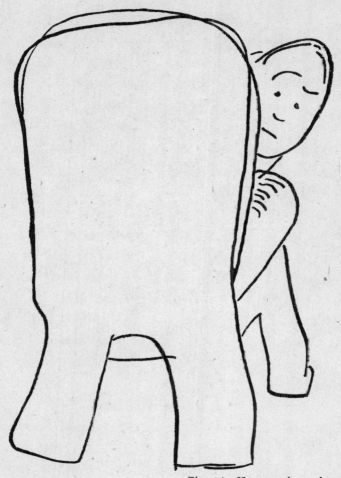

*Fig. 14. Here we have that strange, alert furtiveness which instantly overtakes a man when he beholds a woman doing something which he does not thoroughly understand.*

to doctors that a bearded man,[1] representing the Box Manufacturers, was following him around with a box and trying to catch him. Partly to avoid this imaginary menace, and also partly to stay off imaginary paint, the patient no longer walked on the floor, but on table tops, mantels, and so on, leaping around the room like an oriole. Unless watched, he would jump for the window-sills, and try to get out. He wrote to the Department of Justice at Washington, and finally to the President of the United States, protesting against the activities of the Order of the Eastern Star, the Railway Y. M. C. A., a Rev. W——, and the *New York Times*. The case was decreed hopeless in 1926. Later, the wife got a divorce and the husband seemed to improve. He was permitted to go to a ranch in Dakota, where he had a horse, a dog, and a pipe and was allowed to come and go as he liked. The last time I saw the patient, he was completely cured.

[1] Dr. Prill wore a small, black beard.

## PREVENTION OF NUCLEAR FEARS

Prevention of the nuclear fears which lead to such cases of claustrophobia should be quite simple. A wife should strive at all times to give her husband at least the *illusion* that he is free to come and go. She should remember that it is the little things that count, that claustrophobia is brought on by an accumulation of small details, that it is, in fact, a tragedy of the trivial. If a husband uses a guest towel, he should be quietly reprimanded, but under no circumstances sent to his room. After pointing out, briefly, that the guest towels are not to be used, the wife might even give him a piece of bread and butter with sugar on it, or a kind word. Too many wives do not consider it important to explain the facts of the guest towel to their husbands. A wife expects her husband to pick up his knowledge in the gutter or from other husbands, who know as little about the actual truth as he does himself. If a husband uses a guest towel, he should be gently reproved and

*A wife should tell her hus-*
*band in clear, simple language*
*where guest towels come from.*

then told where guest towels come from, in clear, simple language. The wife should lead him to the drawer where she keeps the guest towels and show him wherein they differ from ordinary towels—the kind he may use. The average guest towel can be identified by curious markings, either elaborate initials or picturesque designs in one corner or running all the way around the border. The husband should also be told that the use of such towels is not pleasurable, because of the discomfort caused by the hemstitching, the rough embroidery, and the like. He should be made to understand that no man ever uses a guest towel, either in his own home or when he is a guest somewhere else, that they are hung up for lady guests to look at and are not to be disturbed. If he is told these simple truths in a calm, unexcited way, the chances are that he will never use a guest towel again and that he won't worry unduly over the consequences of his having used one once or twice. But as soon as he is given the idea that he has done something terrible, that old feeling of being boxed in comes over him. He begins to think that he will never do anything right around the house, and that his home is merely a laboratory in which he has been trapped for the purpose of serving as the subject of strange experiments with towels and furniture.

The same rules should apply to husbands when they leave things lying around, or track in dirt, or forget to shut the refrigerator door. None of these faults is, after all, of very great importance, and they should be lightly dismissed. If they are presented as heinous crimes, the husband is going to be liable to the inception of a Persecution Complex and the slow deterioration of mind and spirit incident upon claustrophobia. A wife is forever taking it for granted that her husband should know as much about a household as she does. If she would only realize that things which are easy and uncomplicated to her are strange and mysterious to her husband, and explain the mysteries to him, adjustments could be arrived at very simply, and sex would then have a chance to mean something. As an instance of what I mean take what happens during the average unpacking. A couple has just moved from one house to another, say, and the husband has been asked to help put things away. (He should not, of course, be asked, for the danger of that boxed-in feeling, with all of its awful consequences, is inherent in such a request.) As the things are taken out of trunks, the wife knows instantly where they go, not only the things she is going to use and wants put where she can get at them, but the things for which she has no immediate use and wishes stored away for the winter or summer, as the case may be. A woman can tell instantly whether a given article belongs in the attic or in the basement. All objects fall into one or the other of these two categories. For example, while I myself am not an expert at it, I am aware that anything framed or having wire attached to it goes to the attic, and that most containers and the like, especially those made of metal, go to the basement. A woman comes naturally by this ability to discriminate. She knows most of it by intuition and the rest she has learned from her mother. But to suppose that a husband should know, offhand, whether a chest of drawers with woolens or dimity in it goes to the attic or the basement is ridiculous. You might as well expect him to understand, without long, careful instruction, why one tea towel is used for the china and another for the glassware. The thing for a wife to do, then, is not to upbraid or rebuff her husband when she finds him tired and worn in the attic, sitting among a lot of things that should have been taken to the basement, but simply to say nothing, or, better yet, compliment him on his strength and agility and then, next day, hire a handy man to shift the things to where they belong. Adherence to a few simple rules of solicitude and understanding would prevent nine husbands out of ten, no matter how passionately dedicated to liberty they may be, from falling victims to the dread claustrophobia which every year takes its heavy toll of male minds as the result of the carelessness or stupidity of wives.

# CHAPTER VIII

## FRIGIDITY IN MEN

I HESITATE to approach the subject of
male unresponsiveness. Frigidity in men
is a theme sociologists have avoided. Frigidity
in women, on the other hand, forms a vast chapter in the sex research of today; the part it plays
in marital discord is known to students of soci-
ology as well as to the lay reader, although probably less well. It has occupied the attention of
many noted writers, and has taken the lives of
such men as Zaner and Tithridge, who carried
some of their experiments too far.[1]

Any discussion of frigidity in men calls for
an unusual degree of frankness on the part of
the writer, since it entails such factors as the
"recessive knee," Fuller's retort, and the declination of the kiss. Further, before attacking this

[1] Tithridge especially.

[ 160 ]

subject, it will be necessary to reëvaluate some of the more fundamental hypotheses of Man's erotic nature, and what a nuisance that is going to be!

Let us go back a little way. There are two fundamental urges in nature: the desire to eat and the desire to reproduce one's kind. Which of these two impulses is the stronger depends somewhat on the individual and somewhat on the circumstances surrounding the individual— that is, it is apt to vary with the quality of the food and of the women. There are, Zaner shows, men who would rather eat than reproduce, and there are isolated cases of men who would rather reproduce than eat. But it is the less simple types that provide the important case histories for the student of masculine frigidity, and no broad conclusions can be drawn about the relative merits of eating and reproducing without a consideration of the contributing factors.

Quite regardless of which urge comes first in Man's scheme of existence, it is safe to state dogmatically that the second urge (the "sex" urge) has caused more stir in the last few years than the first, or "nourishment," urge. Sex is less than fifty years old, yet it has upset the whole Western World. The sublimation of sex, called Love, is of course much older—although many purists will question the existence of Love prior to about 1885 on the grounds that there can be no sublimation of a non-existent feeling. What I shall try to show, without carping, will be that there is a very good reason why the erotic side of Man has called forth so much more discussion lately than has his appetite for food. The reason is this: that while the urge to eat is a personal matter which concerns no one but the person hungry (or, as the German has it, *der hungrig Mensch*), the sex urge involves, for its true expression, another individual. It is this "other individual" that causes all the trouble.

Except in rare instances, all of which have been dealt with by Sumner, the urge involves an individual of the opposite sex; that is, for a man it involves a woman, and for a woman it involves a man. I use the word "involve" advisedly. *Just the minute another person is drawn into some one's life there begin to arise undreamed-of complexities,* and from such a

*"Just the minute another person is drawn into some one's life, there begin to arise undreamed-of complexities."*

simple beginning as sexual desire we find built up such alarming yet familiar phenomena as *fêtes, divertissements,* telephone conversations, arrangements, plans, sacrifices, train arrivals, meetings, appointments, tardinesses, delays, marriages, dinners, small pets and animals, calumny, children, music lessons, yellow shades for the windows, evasions, lethargy, cigarettes, candies, repetition of stories and anecdotes, infidelity, ineptitude, incompatibility, bronchial trouble, and many others, all of which are entirely foreign to the original urge and way off the subject, and all of which make the person's existence so strangely bewildering that if he could have foreseen these developments his choice would have been the "eating" urge, and he would have just gone quietly out somewhere and ordered himself a steak and some French fried potatoes as being the easier way out.

Still, that is just a hypothetical alternative. Life, as we know, is very insistent; almost daily people become involved with other people. And that brings us to our real theme, namely, frigidity in men.

*The Recessive Knee.* The first symptom of frigidity in men is what I call the recessive knee. To the study of this phenomenon I have given some of my best years. My laboratory has been the laboratory of life itself. Probably I would never have discovered the recessive knee had I not noticed it, some ten years ago, in myself. Questioning my colleagues, I found to my amazement that they too had had similar experiences which they were unable to account for, and this led me to continue my investigations. Since then I have gone into taxicabs, terminal lunch rooms, boat liveries, and all other places where it is possible or usual for a girl to let her knee rest lightly against that of her companion, have gained the confidence of the young men and women whom I was watching, and have accumulated a mass of data showing that frigidity in men, instead of being almost a non-existent characteristic, is one of the commonest attributes of our national sexual life. Inasmuch as the juxtaposing of the knee by the female, which causes the recessive (or "pulled away") knee in the male, usually occurs fairly soon after dinner, my experiments and observations have had to be made largely in the evening. It has been my custom to sleep late mornings to make up for this.

Simply stated, the knee phenomenon is this: occasions arise sometimes when a girl presses

*"Occasions arise sometimes when a girl presses her knee, ever so gently, against the knee of the young man she is out with."*

her knee, ever so gently, against the knee of the young man she is out with. The juxtaposing of the knee is brought about by any of a thousand causes. Often the topic of conversation has

something to do with it: the young people, talking along pleasantly, will suddenly experience
a sensation of compatibility, or of friendliness,
or of pity, or of community-of-interests. One
of them will make a remark singularly agreeable
to the other person—a chance word or phrase
that seems to establish a bond between them.
Such a remark can cause the knee of the girl
to be placed against the knee of the young man.
Or, if the two people are in a cab, the turning of
a sharp corner will do it. In canoes, the wash
from a larger vessel will bring it about. In
restaurants and dining-rooms it often takes place
under the table, as though by accident. On
divans, sofas, settees, couches, davenports, and
the like, the slight twist of the young lady's
body incident to receiving a light for her cigarette will cause it. I could go on indefinitely,
but there is no need. It is not a hard push, you
understand—rather the merest touch of knee to
knee, light as the brush of a falling blossom
against one's cheek, and just as lovely.

Now, a normal male in whom there are no

traces of frigidity will allow his knee to retain its original position, sometimes even exerting a very slight counter-pressure. A frigid male, however, will move his knee away at the first suggestion of contact, denying himself the electric stimulus of love's first stirring. Why? That is what my research was conducted to discover. *I found that in 93 per cent of all cases, the male was suspicious; in 4 per cent he was ignorant; and in 3 per cent he was tired.* I have presented these figures to the American Medical Association and am awaiting a reply.

It is the female's subtlety in her laying-on of the knee that annoys the male, I found. His recession is for the purpose of reassuring himself of his own integrity and perspicacity. If the female were to juxtapose in a forthright manner, if she were to preface her gesture with the remark: "I am thinking of letting my knee touch yours for the fun of it, Mortimer," she might gain an entirely different response from the male.

Many men with recessive knees have confided

to me that they felt incapable of answering the pressure because of the effect it might have on their minds, with the accompanying loss of self-respect. I have established the fact that no *physical* detriment is incurred by answered pressure—the only harmful effects are psychological. Some males admitted to an unwillingness to give any woman the satisfaction of believing that she was able to take her companion unaware. Still others told me that they feared the consequences of such an act: they were afraid that if ever they let down the bars and failed to turn away from knee pressure, they would likewise be unable to resist other juxtapositions in life and would continually be responding amiably to other amusing stimuli—sales talks, stock promotion, and the like.

It was a young Paterson, N. J., girl by the name of Lillian Fuller who let drop the remark that has epitomized, for the sociological and anthropological world, the phenomenon of the recessive knee. "Fuller's retort" is now a common phrase in the realm of psychotherapy.

Miss Fuller was an unusually beautiful woman—young, accurate, sensitive. She was greatly attached to a man several years her senior in the buffing department; wanted to marry him. To this end she had laid her knee against his innumerable times without a single return of pressure. His frigidity, she realized, was gradually becoming prejudicial to his mental health, and so one evening, after experiencing for the hundredth time the withdrawal of his knee, she simply turned to him with a quiet smile playing on her face and said, "Say, what is the matter with you, anyway?"

Her retort somehow summed up the whole question of frigidity in men.

*The Declination of the Kiss.*[1] Many men have told me that they would not object to sex were it not for its contactual aspect. That is, they said they would be perfectly willing to express their eroticism if it could be done at a reasonable distance—say fifty paces. These men (the frigid-*plus* type) found kissing intolerable.

[1] Now we're getting down to business.

"Many men have told me that they would not object to sex were it not for its contactual aspect." (One such man is shown in the background.)

When they had an opportunity to kiss a young lady, they declined. They made it plain that they would be willing to blow a kiss across the room from their hand, but not execute it with their lips.

I analyzed scores of these cases, questioning both the women and the men. (The women were mad as hornets.) I found that a small number of the kiss-declining men were suffering from a pathology of the eyes—either astigmatism or farsightedness—so that when they got really close to a girl, she blurred on them.[1] The vast majority of cases, however, were quite different. Their unwillingness I traced to a much subtler feeling than eye-strain. Your true anti-contactual, or kiss-decliner, is a very subtle individual indeed.

In effect, he is a throw-back to another period in history, specifically to the Middle Ages. He is a biological sport. (Note: this is very confusing, calling him a "sport," because the

[1] Incidentally, I might say that this blurring of the female before the eyes of the male is not entirely unpleasant. It's kind of fun.

[ 173 ]

ordinary "sport" is not a kiss-decliner at all—
anything but. Please keep in mind, then, that
when I use the term "sport" I want the strict
biological interpretation put upon the word. I

*"Love had a simple directness which was not disturbed
until the arrival, in the land, of the minnesingers."*

want it, and I intend to get it. If there are any
of you who think you are going to find the use
of the word "sport" in this connection so confusing as to make the rest of the chapter unin-
telligible, I wish you would drop out. Get

something else to read, or, better yet, get some exercise.)

No one can quite comprehend the motives and the successes of a kiss-decliner who does not recall his counterpart in mediæval history. In the Middle Ages, when men were lusty and full of red meat, their women expected as much. A baronial fellow, finishing his meal, made no ado about kissing a Middle Age woman. He just got up from the table and kissed her. Bango, and she was kissed. Love had a simple directness which was not disturbed until the arrival, in the land, of the *minnesingers*. It got so no baronial hall of the Middle Ages was free from these *minnesingers*. They kept getting in. They would bring their harps with them, and after dinner they would twang a couple of notes and then sing a frail, delicate song to the effect that women should be worshiped from afar, rather than possessed. To a baron who had just drunk a goblet of red wine, this new concept of womanhood was screamingly funny. While he was chuckling away to himself and cutting himself another side of beef, his wife, who had listened attentively to the song, would slip out into the alley behind the castle and there the *minnesinger* would join her.

*Mediæval baron, amused at minnesinger's concept of Woman.*

"Sing that one again," she would say.

"Which one?"

"That one about worshiping me from a little distance. I want to hear that one again."

The *minnesinger* would oblige. Then he would illustrate the theme by *not* kissing the woman, but dancing off lightly down the hill, throwing his harp up into the air and catching it again as he went.

"What a nice young man," the baron's wife would think, as she slowly turned and went in to bed.

The kiss-decliner of today is a modern *minnesinger*. He is a sport in that he has varied suddenly from the normal type—which is still baronial. Of course, the amusing thing about his conduct is that oftentimes a woman assumes that she is being worshiped from afar, when as a matter of fact she is merely being *ignored from afar*. That is part of the trick of an anti-contactual person—he takes a perverse delight in allowing the woman whose kiss he has declined, to think of him as more lyrical than other men. When he leaves her presence, she is apt to think of him as off somewhere by the bank of a stream, lying flat on his back, his shaggy head buried in the tall grasses, dreaming of something or other

·—probably of her, whereas, if she would take the trouble to go to the nearest Liggett's drug store she would probably find him there, getting a sundæ.

By the mere gesture of declining a kiss a man can still make quite a lot of ground, even in these depleted days. The woman thinks: "He would not dream of embracing my body; now that's pretty white of him!" Of course, it would be wrong to ascribe motives of sheer deliberateness to the frigid male. Often he is not a bad sort—merely is a fellow who prefers an imagined kiss to the real kind. An imagined kiss is more easily controlled, more thoroughly enjoyed, and less cluttery than an actual kiss. To kiss in dream is wholly pleasant. First, the woman is the one of your selection, not just anyone who happens to be in your arms at the moment. Second, the deed is garnished with a little sprig of glamour which the mind, in exquisite taste, contributes. Third, the lips, imaginatively, are placed just so, the right hand is placed just so, the concurrent thoughts arrive, just so. Except for the fact that the whole episode is a little bit stuffy, it is a superior experience all round. When a kiss becomes actual, anything is likely to happen. The lips, failing of the mark, may strike lightly against the end of the lady's nose, causing the whole adventure to crack up; or the right hand may come in contact with the hard, jagged part of the shoulder blade; or, worst of all, the man's thoughts may not clothe the moment with the proper splendor: he may be worrying about something.

So you see, frigidity in men has many aspects, many angles. To me it is vastly more engrossing than frigidity in women, which is such a simple phenomenon you wonder anybody bothers about it at all.

# ANSWERS TO HARD QUESTIONS

[Note: These questions have been selected from among the many thousand inquiries that were received by Dr. Karl Zaner during the past year. They come from people who are sexually inquisitive—people from every walk of life. The authors wish to thank Dr. Zaner for allowing them to have access to his sex files. It is with a sense of high adventure that we face the task of answering, to the best of our ability, these perplexing questions that deal so intimately with human lives.—THE AUTHORS.]

*Q. My youngest boy, age 28, turned against love because in a book he was reading, where the writer meant to say, "A woman in love is sacred" there was a misprint and it came out, "A woman in love is scared." How would you go about this?*

*A.* We do not regard the case as typical. Presumably your boy is badly frightened himself, or he wouldn't be reading books; he would be out somewhere. The way to overcome this is to build up his general health.

*Q. Should a woman live with her husband if they are separated?*

*A.* Yes. There is nothing that brings two people so close together as separation. In situations of the sort, the woman's presence gradually becomes necessary on account of the condition of the man's shirts. On first being separated from his wife, the husband commonly will be found to neglect his dirty clothes, from spite and from self-indulgence. Instead of gathering them into a pile and sending them to a laundry, he will put on yesterday's shirt in the morning, and stop in a gentleman's furnishing store to pick up a clean one on the way to the office. This procedure has a threefold allure for the man. First, it gets him to the office half an hour late; second, it takes him into a furnishing store; and third, when he looks into his shirt drawer in the morning and finds no shirts it assures him of the disorganized state of his life. To feel disorganized is to be perfectly happy.

Things might go on this way indefinitely were it not for the economic side of the question. At three dollars a shirt (which is a conservative figure for a man separated from his wife) the shirt bill runs into eighteen dollars a week, plus another six dollars for underwear and socks. Furthermore, there is now a congested condition in the husband's office, caused by the accumulation of dirty shirts which he has tucked into bottom drawers and filing cabinets. This shows up in his work.

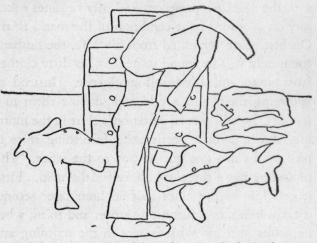

*"On first being separated from his wife, the husband commonly will be found to neglect his dirty clothes, from spite and from self-indulgence. Instead of gathering them into a pile and sending them to the laundry, he will put on yesterday's shirt in the morning, and stop in a gentlemen's furnishing store to pick up a clean one on the way to the office."*

The impracticability of two people living apart becomes apparent, too, in the matter of the old 1916 Cadillac touring car which they own. On separating, the husband will generously give the car to his wife to use, but that doesn't alter the fact that he, and he alone, knows what you have to do when the car "does that funny thing." Thus, the husband is apt any time during the day to pick up the phone and hear his wife's voice:

"Dear, I'm on the Merrick Road between Bellport and Patchogue, and the car is doing that funny thing again." This means dropping whatever work he is doing, taking a cab to the Penn station and a Long Island train to the scene of the breakdown. This also shows up in his work. It never could happen if husband and wife were living together, because in that case they would never be on cordial enough terms for him to let her use the car.

There is another phase of separation that is perhaps more alarming than those we have mentioned, namely, the possible effect the news of it might have on the health of the wife's parents or the health of the husband's parents. I recall the case of a couple who over a period of years tried to live apart without telling the wife's mother—who had a frail heart and who liked to see young people together, not apart. (Note: old ladies don't know *why* they like to see young people together—they can give no reason; yet just the thought of two young people separating excites them unduly, and,

[ 183 ]

when their heart is unreliable, is apt to carry them off.) So this young pair, out of consideration, although separated, sent community Christmas presents to the parents and wrote letters describing joint experiences, until, after two years and eight months of struggling along and scheming, they finally gave up the battle and decided it would be simpler to take an apartment together somewhere. Sheer fatigue united them. They are residing, to this day, in North Pelham, and the wife's mother is still alive and well. Getting better every day, doctors say.

So our advice to any couple is just this: separate if you must, but by all means live together—no matter how your friends and neighbors talk.

*Q. I have an aquarium and I got a snail for it because they told me it would keep the water clean, and the snail unexpectedly bore young, although it was in there all alone. I mean there weren't any other snails in there, only fish. How could it have young, very well?*

*A.* The snail in your aquarium is a mollusc. It is quite likely an hermaphrodite, even though it came from a reputable department store. For being hermaphroditic, nobody can blame a snail. We cannot tell you everything we know about the gastropods because we know, possibly, more than is good for us. In the absence of specific information to the contrary, we would say that the snail in your aquarium had been going around a good deal with other snails before you got him (her). Some molluscs (not many) can have children merely by sitting around and thinking about it. Others can have children by living in a state of reciprocity with other hermaphrodites. Still others are like us, diœcious, possessed of only one sexual nature but thankful for small favors.

The shellfish and the snails are a great group, though it is a pose with many people to consider them dull. Usually the people who find molluscs dull are dull themselves. We have met molluscs in many parts of the world: in gardens in France, on the rocks at low tide on Long Island Sound, in household aquaria, on the sidewalks of suburban towns in the early mornings, in restaurants, and in forests. Everywhere we found them to be sensitive creatures, imaginative and possessed of a lively sense of earth's pleasant rhythm. Snails have a kind of nobility. Zoölogists will tell you that they occupy, in the animal kingdom, a position of enviable isolation. They go their own way.

We can understand your curiosity about sex in snails. Molluscs are infinitely varied in their loves, their hates, and their predilections. They have a way of carrying out ideas they get in their head. They are far from cold, as many people suppose them; indeed, one of the most fascinating love stories we ever read was in the *Cambridge Natural History,* in which was described the tryst kept by a pair of snails on a garden wall. We have never forgotten the first sentence of that romantic and idyllic tale, nor have we forgotten the name of the snail, L. Maximus. The story started: "L. Maximus has been observed at midnight to ascend a wall or some perpendicular surface." It then went on to relate how, after some moments spent greeting each other, crawling round and round, the snails let themselves down on a little ladder of their own devising, and there, suspended in the air ten inches or so from the top of the wall, they found love.

Often very fecund, molluscs are rarely too busy to give attention to their children after birth, or to prepare for their coming. There is, in Algeria, a kind of mollusc whose young return for shelter to the body of their mother, somewhat in the manner of little kangaroos. There is, in the Philippines, a snail who is so solicitous for her expected babies that she goes to the trouble of climbing, with infinite pains and no little discomfort, to the top of a tall tree, and there deposits her eggs in a leaf, folding the leaf adroitly for protection. Another kind of mollusc, having laid her eggs upon a stone, amuses herself by arranging them like the petals of a rose, and hatches them by holding her foot on them. Molluscs tend to business.

Sometimes different species intermarry, but this is rare. The interesting point about it is that such unions generally take place when the air is heavily charged with electricity, as before a storm, or when great rains have made the earth wet. The Luxembourg Garden in Paris is a place snails go to for clandestine matches of this sort. H. Variabilis goes there, and Pisana. The moisture, the electricity, the fragrant loveliness of a Paris night, stir them strangely.

Probably, if you know so little of the eroticism of snails, you have not heard of the darts some of them carry—tiny daggers, hard and sharp, with which they prick each other for the excitement it affords. These darts are made of carbonate of lime. The Germans call them *Liebespfeil,* "love shaft." Many British molluscs are without them, but that's the way it goes.

## IS SEX NECESSARY?

We could tell much more. We could tell about molluscs that possess the curious property of laying their eggs on the outside of their own shell, and of the strange phenomenon of the Cephalopod, who, when he takes leave of his lady, leaves one of his arms with her, so that she may never lack for an embrace. But we feel we have answered your question.

# GLOSSARY

AARON'S DISEASE: Put in here merely because it might confuse the reader if we started right off with Admiral Schley.

ADMIRAL SCHLEY: American naval hero in whose splendid achievements men took an interest when their absorption in love died down, *circa* 1900.

AMATORY INSTINCTS: Interest in sex.

APATHY: Almost total loss of interest in sex.

ATROPHY: Total loss of interest in sex.

ATTACK: Man's method of showing interest in women, so called because of his brusque desire to get at the matter in hand and have done with it.

BEGONIA-ISM: Tendency of the male to raise small potted plants, and not go out.

BENIGN STUPOR: Alarming condition in a husband or lover which causes him to sit around in his bathrobe and slippers, brooding, instead of working or anything.

BIOLOGICO-CULTURAL: A feminine type; one who expresses her erotic nature verbally.

BOTHER: Annoyance; frequently confused with "pother," which means uncalled-for interest in something, usually sex.

BOXED-IN: Caught, or trapped, as a husband by a wife, or the delusion of being caught or trapped.

BUTCHER'S TWINE: A kind of stout cord of no particular interest to anybody.

CAUSATION: The factors back of a male's doubt or suspicion.

CHARADES: (1) Parlor game devised by women to fend off men (1900-1909); (2) acting up in a skittish manner about the facts of life, instead of getting right down to them; twitching, nervous twitching.

COMPLEX: Mental crack-up caused by an emotional, or physical, inability to get away from, or wind things up with, a person of the opposite sex.

COMPLEX, NUCLEAR: Shock caused by discovery of a person of the opposite sex in his or her true colors; beginning of a general breakdown.

DEFENSE: Feminine excuses, tricks, devices, etc.

DELAY MECHANISM: Pother.

DETERIORATION (BENIGN): Going quietly to pieces as the result of marriage or a love affair.

# GLOSSARY

DETERIORATION (MALIGNANT): Going loudly to pieces under the same circumstances; fidgeting, bawling, berating, etc.

DIVERSION SUBTERFUGE: Trick employed by women to keep men's minds on ethereal, rather than physical, matters.

EMPIRIC: National viewpoint of sex.

EROTIC: Of or pertaining to sex, usually in a pretty far-fetched manner.

EXHIBITIONISM: Going too far, but not really meaning it.

EXOTIC: Of an alarming nature, particularly to parents.

FIXATION: Too great dependence on one woman.

FRAGMENTATION OF PERSONALITY: Inception of general decline on the part of the male.

FRIGIDITY (in men): Suspicion, ignorance, or fatigue, mostly suspicion.

FUDGE-MAKING: Feminine trick or device.

FULLER'S RETORT: A remark made by a Paterson, N. J., girl one night in Paterson, N. J.

GEORGE SMITH: A despondent Indianapolis real-estate man. Pulling a George Smith: attempting to find something more important than, and just as interesting as, women.

JULIA MARLOWE: Actress.

LIBIDO: "Pleasure-principle."

LOOSENESS OF SYSTEMATIZATION: The going to pieces of a husband.

LOVE: The pleasant confusion which we know exists.

LOVING: Being confused by, or confusing some one.

MASCULINE PROTEST: Male disdain for things which he does not understand.

NARCISSISM: Attempt to be self-sufficient, with overtones.

NEURO-VEGETATIVE REFLEXES: A male's, particularly a husband's, quick, unpremeditated reactions to stewed vegetables, especially spinach, and to certain salads.

NEUROSIS: The beginning of the end, unless the husband can go away somewhere.

NEUROTIC: Wanting something, but she doesn't know what; desirous of something she hasn't got and probably can't, or shouldn't, have.

1907, PANIC OF: Result of woman's inhumanity to man (1900-1907).

NO BETTER THAN SHE OUGHT TO BE (woman's definitions): (1) indiscreet; (2) charming; (3) pretty and vivacious; (4) oversexed; (5) living in sin.

NORM: All Quiet.

NUMERICAL PROTECTION: Other people in the room.

# GLOSSARY

OSCULATORY JUSTIFICATION: Reasons for kissing, growing out of the early American credo that kissing for kissing's sake would send one straight to hell.

PARANOIA: The last stages of what was once a bridegroom.

PASSION: Expression of the sex principle without so much fuss.

PEDESTALISM: The American male's reverence for the female or, better yet, her insistence on being revered, which amounts to the same thing.

PHYSICO-PSYCHIC: State in which the physical gets tangled up with the spiritual, after the manner of a setter pup throwing a huntsman by getting between his feet.

PLEASURE-PRINCIPLE: See Libido.

POSSESSIVE COMPLEX: Innocent desire to kiss and fondle, sometimes to maul or wool.

POTHER: Uncalled-for interest in something—almost always sex.

PROTECTIVE REACTION: Putting a man in his place.

PSYCHE: Wings for the feet of clay.

PSYCHO-NEUROSIS: Same as neurosis, only worse.

PSYCHOSIS: State of being beside oneself to such an extent that it is doubtful if one can pull oneself together.

PULLED-AWAY: Refers to the knee of a man who is suspicious or tired.

RECESSIVE KNEE: The outstanding phenomenon of masculine frigidity; man's refusal to answer the pressure.

SCHMALHAUSEN, SAMUEL D.: Student of misbehavior.

SCHMALHAUSEN TROUBLE: Illness commonly found in young ladies who read in cramped quarters.

SMITH, GEORGE: Same as George Smith.

SWASTIKA: Symbol which distracted American suitors used to scrawl on desk pads, margins of books, and so on.

TROUBLE, SCHMALHAUSEN: See Schmalhausen trouble.

ÜBERTRAGUNG: Period of transition during which the male strives to transmute his ardor for women into the semblance of ardor for games.

VOYEURISM: Sex Kibitzing.

# A NOTE ON THE DRAWINGS IN THIS BOOK

The inclusion, in this volume, of some fifty-two drawings by James Thurber, was on the whole intentional. Because, however, of the strong feeling of suspicion which they will arouse in certain quarters, it may not be amiss to offer some explanation. For this task I feel peculiarly fitted, for it was I who, during those trying months when the book was in the making, picked up the drawings night after night from the floor under Thurber's desk, picked them up when I was so tired in body and soul that I could scarcely stoop; it was I who, by gaining the confidence of the charwomen, nightly redeemed countless other thousands of unfinished sketches from the huge waste baskets; and finally, it was my incredible willingness to go through with the business of "inking-in" the drawings (necessitated by the fact that they were done in such faint strokes of a broken pencil as to be almost invisible to the naked eye) that at last brought them to the point where they could be engraved and reproduced.

To understand, even vaguely, Thurber's art, it is necessary to grasp the two major themes which underlie all his drawings. The first theme is what I call the "melancholy of sex"; the other is what I can best describe as the "implausibility of animals." These two basic ideas motivate, subconsciously, his entire creative life. Just how some of the animals shown in these pages "come in" is not clear even to me—except in so far as any animal must be regarded as sexually relevant because of our human tendency to overestimate what can be learned from watching it.

When one studies the drawings, it soon becomes apparent that a strong undercurrent of grief runs through them. In almost every instance the *man* in the picture is badly frightened, or even hurt. These "Thurber men" have come to be recognized as a distinct type in the world of art; they are frustrated, fugitive beings; at times they seem vaguely striving to get out of something without being seen (a room, a situation, a state of mind), at other times they are merely perplexed and too humble, or weak, to move. The *women,* you will notice, are quite different: temperamentally they are much better adjusted to their surroundings than are the men, and mentally they are much less capable of making themselves uncomfortable.

It would be foolish to attempt here a comprehensive appreciation of the fierce sweep, the economy, and the magnificent obscurity of Thurber's work, nor can I adequately indicate the stark qualities in the drawings that have earned for him the title of "the Ugly Artist." All I, all anybody, can do is to hint at the uncanny faithfulness with which he has caught—caught and thrown to the floor—the daily, indeed the almost momently, severity of life's mystery, as well as the charming doubtfulness of its purpose.

E. B. W.

# May B.

### A Novel

### by Caroline Starr Rose

schwartz & wade books · new york

Text copyright © 2012 by Caroline Starr Rose
Jacket art copyright © 2012 by Christopher Silas Neal

Visit us on the Web! www.randomhouse.com/kids

Educators and librarians, for a variety of teaching tools, visit us at
www.randomhouse.com/teachers

Library of Congress Cataloging-in-Publication Data
Rose, Caroline Starr.
May B. : a novel-in-verse / by Caroline Starr Rose.—1st ed.
p. cm.
Summary: When a failed wheat crop nearly bankrupts the Betterly
family, Pa pulls twelve-year-old May from school and hires
her out to a couple new to the Kansas frontier.
ISBN 978-1-58246-393-3 (hardcover) — ISBN 978-1-58246-412-1
(gibraltar library binding) — ISBN 978-1-58246-437-4 (ebook)
[1. Novels in verse. 2. Frontier and pioneer life—Kansas—Fiction.
3. Kansas—History—19th century—Fiction.] I. Title.
PZ7.5.R67May 2011
[Fic]—dc22
2010033222

The text of this book is set in 12.5-point Archetype.
Book design by Rachael Cole

Printed in the United States of America
10 9 8 7 6 5 4 3 2 1

First Edition

In loving memory of my grandmother,
Gene Starr Craig


For my students in New Mexico, Florida, Virginia, and
Louisiana: There are a few of you whose needs I didn't
fully understand and others I could have done better by.
This story is for you.

# Part One

I won't go.

"It's for the best," Ma says,
yanking to braid my hair,
trying to make something of what's left.

Ma and Pa want me to leave
and live with strangers.

I won't go.

"It's for the best,
you packing up and moving
to the Oblingers' soddy."
Ma's brush tugs.
My eyes sting.

For the best,
like when the Wright baby died,
not three weeks old—
one less child to clothe.

After all,
I cook some,
collect fuel,
mend,
tote water,
hoe,
wash,
pretty braid or not.

Why not Hiram? I think,
but I already know:
boys are necessary.

"You'll bring in some extra money," Ma says.

"We'll get you home by Christmas."
A wisp of hair escapes her grasp,
encircling my cheek.

For the best,
one less child to clothe.

Before Ma ties my ribbon,
I push outside and run.
My feet pound out
I won't go
I won't go
I won't go.

My braid spills loose.
The short pieces hang about one ear.
Hiram—
the hunk of hair he cut
because I dared him to.
He got his lashing
like we knew he would,
his smile full of pride.
Why didn't he cut it all?
Then maybe,
like Samson in the Bible,
I'd be useless too.

I stop when home is nothing more
than a mound on the windswept plain.
Like a prairie hen I settle down
until I can't be seen,
breathing comfort from grass and soil.
I listen for silence,
but there's no room for it.
My mind's too full.
Ma and Pa want me to leave
and live with strangers.

Around my finger
I twist a blade of grass.
It's what I've always wanted,
to contribute,
but not this way.
If I leave,
schooling is as good as finished.
Come Christmas I'll be home
but even farther
behind.

In three more years
I'll be old enough.
In three more years

maybe
I'll be able to teach.

I grab a fistful of shorn hair.
I *am* no better than Samson
once that Delilah cut his hair,
once his strength was gone.
Powerless.
Defeated.

Mavis Elizabeth Betterly
May Betts
May B.

Somehow Hiram spots me.
"What're you hiding for?" he asks.
I stand up and punch him on the arm,
for cutting my hair,
for being a boy,
for reading strong,
easy as you please.
I punch him again.

Hiram rubs his shoulder,
then hooks his arm through mine.
"Ma asked me to fetch you.
Suppertime."

Our soddy's dark and smells like the prairie
with its freshness stolen away.
Ma's laid the table;
Pa's boots are near the door.

I tuck my hair behind my ears
and sit down with Hiram.
"Ma told you?" Pa asks
straight after grace.
"Better pack tonight."

I nod,
stare down at the chicken fixings
(no everyday salt pork tonight).
Ma's even set out tinned peaches.

"The homestead's fifteen miles west of here,"
   Pa says.
"The bride's not settled,
got here after Oblinger built his soddy."
Pa looks at me.
"She's missing home."

Won't I miss home?
Ma touches my hand.

"It's just till Christmas, May."

I push away,
my peaches left untouched.

# 7

Once the table's cleared and Hiram's out with
   Pa,
Ma opens her hope chest.
She unfolds her finest pillowcase
and slips my Sunday dress inside.
She adds her old calico,
worn a yellow-brown,
and a chemise
made by her own ma.

"You'll need some shoes."
Ma pulls out boots I rarely see,
dainty and ladylike.
I'm to leave Hiram's old pair for her.

Three dresses,
counting my work dress.
Ma's chemise,
along with my own.
Two sets of stockings.
Two pairs of bloomers.
Two aprons.
My coat.
Woolen mittens.
New shoes.

I pull the crate from under my bed,
taking my reader and my slate.

Ma sighs. "Ain't no way you'll keep up
with the rest."
"I know," I say.

I catch what's not said:
it's foolishness to keep pretending.
What sort of teacher can't read out lessons?

*Maybe May B. can*
*Maybe May B. can't*

I remember when we first came
what Pa used to say.
"Hiram and you are as young as Kansas.
As fresh to life
as the Prairie State."

Those traveling weeks we watched the sky
from the wagon
or walking beside it,
hoping to be the first to spy
the distant place where
the ground and air connect.
This became our game,
Hiram's and mine,
and once on our land,
farther west than ever before,
we stood
on the gentle rise
where the coneflowers and wild mustard
   bloom.
Wind cutting my eyes,
I searched for
that place where land touches sky.

# 9

While Pa fetches the wagon in the early-
     morning black,
Hiram pulls me around back.
He doesn't need to tell me
we're going to the gentle rise
where wildflowers grow.

Hiram and I stand high
as the countryside allows.
Behind us,
there's the smallest hint of sun.

"Remember, May Betts,
it's just beyond."
Hiram points into the darkness,
like I might forget.
We haven't seen it yet,
but we know it's there.

Pa's taking me farther west,
toward sunset and rain,
farther from town than Hiram's ever been.

I hold out my hand.
"If I see it first,

you owe me your Christmas candy.
If you see it, I'll give you mine."
Hiram's fingers squeeze my hand. "Agreed."

"How do I know you'll be honest?" I say.
He squints at me.
"I wouldn't lie.
That takes the fun out of winning."

Hiram's better at races,
always grabs the extra biscuit.
Ma's first spring baby,
he beat me to living
by one short year.
And now,
for once,
I'll be ahead.

"Maybe I'll see it first," I say.
Hiram tags me
fast,
then starts to run home.
"Or maybe not!" he tosses back.

Our mare pulls,
the wagon sways,
the grass ripples.
Only I am holding back.

Pa's hunched over the reins.
I wonder when he'll speak his piece.
Since last night's supper he's been
silent.

I find myself inside the rhythm
of hoof
and wheel
and join this going forward,
but I am behind, still.

I play a game inside my head,
counting plum trees that dot a creek bed,
rabbits that scatter at the sound of wagon
   wheels,
clouds that skirt the sky.
For hours, that is all,
and grass,
always grass,
in different shades and textures
like the braids in a rag rug.

Miss Sanders told us that lines never end,
and numbers go on forever.
Here,
in short-grass country,
I understand infinity.

We stop just once to eat,
after the sun has reached its peak.
I watch a bird balance
on a blade of grass
bent low toward earth
to find a meal.
All creatures must work for their keep.

"I know schooling's what you want,
but with this spring's wheat . . ."
Pa shrugs.

"Will Hiram go back?"
I have to know.
He's thirteen now,
one of the oldest boys
still learning.

Pa's eyes meet mine.
"No," he says,
"I'll need his help around the place."
I shut my eyes,
catch Hiram's smile.
All term he's complained.
wanting to be a man and work the farm.

"You're helping out, May," Pa says.
I'm helping everyone
except myself.

I see the homestead first:
an awkward lump of earth,
a lazy curl of smoke above.
Beyond the soddy,
a barn carved into a hill.
Pa doesn't need to point but does.
"It's not as nice as what we've got.
Did most of his work alone.
Still plenty of time for improvements."

Pa cut our strips of sod.
He and Ma stacked them,
layer by layer,
grass side down,
using only a bit of precious wood to frame
our windows and door.

This soddy's small,
the earthen walls misshapen,
just one papered window.

I clutch my pillowcase.

Mr. Oblinger spies us,
waves,

steps inside his home.
Later,
when we're closer,
I catch the flaming red of Mrs. Oblinger's
    dress.
She stands in the doorway for a time,
facing us.
It's only when we approach
that she shuts herself inside.

# 14

I stay in the wagon,
watching Pa and Mr. Oblinger
inspect the garden,
point toward empty prairie.
Without hearing,
I know the talk
of plow,
of wheat,
of rain
and promise.

Hand passes to hand,
and Pa tucks money
inside his shirt pocket.

It's then he motions toward me.
I can't pretend not to see.

Pa gives my shoulders a gentle squeeze.
"This here's Mavis."
"May," I say.
"Glad to have you with us, May."
Mr. Oblinger shakes Pa's hand.
"You sure you don't want to stay?"
"No, thank you," Pa says.

"We need provisions from town.
I'll sleep there tonight."

Pa pulls me close,
the crisp money crackles
against my cheek.
My first wage.
"Till Christmas," he says.
"Do your best."

I nod.

But I know
my best isn't always good enough.

## 15

I don't wait until Pa's far
before I turn toward the door.
Watching him
would only stretch the distance.

Just a push swings the door open.
The air inside is heavy
with heat,
with darkness,
with something I can't name.

Mrs. Oblinger turns,
her skirts
swirl,
her eyes
study me like a lesson.
She's fancy and tall,
but I've caught it right away—
she's hardly older than I.

"This here's where you'll sleep."
She holds out her arm,
like showing me
a spot vast as the prairie.
Not a hint of privacy—

a dingy corner,
muslin pinned across the ceiling
stained brown
from rain that seeps through the sod.
I stand straight.
"Thank you, ma'am."

Mrs. Oblinger slices the air with one finger.
"Use this crate for your belongings."

She catches my glance at the ceiling,
the sagging cloth already filled with bits of
    soil.
I drop my chin,
study my shoes.

"You'll be no wetter than the rest of us," she
    says.

# 16

"Once you unpack,
you can start in on supper."
I wait for her to turn away,
so I might have one moment to myself.
Mrs. Oblinger doesn't budge.

From the pillowcase,
I pull Ma's calico.
My reader tumbles to the floor.
Mrs. Oblinger scoops it up,
opens the cover slowly,
touches the place I've written my name.
I rip it from her hands and hold it to my chest.

"What was that for?" she demands.
"It's mine," I say.
"Careful, young lady." She flings the words,
more girl than woman herself.

My apology spills out.
"I won't let my schoolwork interfere with
    chores."

Mrs. Oblinger's eyes meet mine.

"I was under the impression you
couldn't read a thing.
Once you unpack,
start in on supper."

I dump my belongings in a pile,
yank off Ma's fancy boots,
my toes more comfortable on the hard-packed
    earth.
My reader and slate I wrap in the pillowcase
and slide them as far under the bed as I can.

I roll out biscuits on the table,
then fix the coffee.
From the garden,
Mr. Oblinger brings cabbage.
"I thought this might round out the meal."
He's got the kind of patchy beard
that says he's new
to prairie living.

Though small,
the cupboard holds
sacks
and
tins.
Mr. Oblinger's been busy,
providing for his bride.

I lay the table,
waiting.
The biscuits grow cold.
I stand at the door,
wave to Mr. Oblinger near the dugout barn.
"The missus inside?" he asks.
I shake my head.

He wipes his face with a handkerchief.
"Wonder where she's gone off to."
Heading to the creek,
he calls for her.
The empty prairie says nothing.
I pretend to study
cabbage,
beans,
a row of potatoes.

Inside I serve up salt pork,
pour coffee,
and wait.

At last
the two walk in.
"Daydreaming out back."

Mr. Oblinger's smile stretches too wide.

Mrs. Oblinger sits,
says nothing.

In bed I think through presidents
and work long division in my head.
It is dark
and quiet,
and the heavy air remains.

# 20

I wake to the gray of early dawn
and stay silent as sleep,
so as not to rouse the Oblingers.
But there's no need:
I'm not the only one awake.

The sound is muffled,
like a child at her mother's shoulder.
Just as Hiram can't hold back laughter during
    family prayers,
Mrs. Oblinger's sobs escape the blankets.

Surely Mr. Oblinger hears?
Three of us awake,
two pretending sleep.

Mr. Oblinger stirs,
I duck farther under my sheet,
and, once he's gone,
slip into my work dress.

Relieved to find the water's low,
I grab the bucket.
Outside I breathe in sunshine,
taking care
not to spend
more time than necessary,
but still walking
slowly enough
to study
sky
and
sweep of land,
postponing
the time when I must enter
that closed-in space.

She sits,
her red dress wrinkled,
smoothing tangles from her hair.
I lower the bucket,
straighten,
allowing my shoulders to relax.

"What's that for?" Her eyes accuse me.
"We were out of water," I try.
"Not that," she says.
"Why'd you sigh?"

"I didn't realize—"

"This work too much for you?"
"No, ma'am."
Her eyebrows rise.
"Did you misplace your boots?"
"Mostly I go barefoot,
except for church or snowy days."
"Truly?" she asks.
There is no need to answer.
She can see for herself.

She returns to brushing.

"What happened to your hair?"
I touch my braid,
unraveling.
"My brother cut it on a dare," I say.

She turns away while twisting her curls into a
    bun.
I hear her just the same.
"Stupid girl."

I busy myself at the stove,
put the coffee on,
start in on biscuits,
wonder what Hiram's doing this morning.

Anytime Ma fried up bacon
and turned away from the stove,
Hiram would make a beeline,
grab a piece from the pan,
drop it with a yelp,
suck on his burned fingers.
One morning he pierced a strip with a fork
and waved it to cool,
flinging globs of slippery grease on Ma's
    curtains.
She swatted him with the broom,
shooing him out the door
like an unwelcome badger.

Now Hiram must wait outside until bacon
    frying's done.

Ma's probably rolling dough,
humming.
Maybe Hiram's grinding coffee

now that I'm not there to help.
He's already brought the milk pail in.
When Pa gets back,
he'll share what he heard in town.

I glance up at Mrs. Oblinger,
silent in her rocker,
and turn back to my biscuits,
thankful to be occupied.

Mrs. Oblinger stands when her husband
    enters.
Her hairbrush slips to the ground.
He bends to pick it up
and hands it to her.
"Sorry for the dust.
Once the puncheon floor's in . . ."
He signals toward the door.
"Chapman's got extra wood at his place.
We'll work on it next week."
She lifts her face.
What light there is
brightens her eyes.
"Thank you," she says.

The coffee is bitter,
the biscuits are hard,
the bath water's cold.
Mrs. Oblinger complains but doesn't help.
How did she manage before now?

It's curious.
How am I to know
what to do
when no one is about
much of the time?
Am I to track down the missus
or force Mr. Oblinger
to stop his work?
Or do I act like I am
the one
ordering this household?

Like a shadow,
Mrs. Oblinger floats about,
sometimes outside,
sometimes in.
Is she at the creek fetching water?

This is not my home.
I am the stranger
here.

Beans cook on the stove,
the beds are neat,
the table laid.
I am alone,
my reader before me.

On days I finished chores early,
Ma would let me work lessons before supper.
I'd curl up in the rocker,
my feet tucked under me,
ignoring Ma's scolding
to sit like a lady.
Hiram would perch at the end of his bed,
his elbows on his knees,
my reader in his hands:

*"The Grandeur of the Sea"*

*What is there more sublime than the trackless,
restless, unfathomable sea? What is there
grander than the calm, gently-heaving,
silent sea?*

With my eyes shut tight,
I'd see the swirling waters,

feel the sea's smooth coolness.
Hiram went over lessons
until I knew them through.
Only then
would I slip into the barn
and try to read what I'd heard to Bessie
until Ma called me for supper.

Mrs. Oblinger comes through the door,
focusing on me,
not one glance at the work I've done.
She opens her mouth as if to speak.
Without a word I close my book;
she turns and walks away.

I think on what Mrs. Oblinger said when I
    first came.
How did she hear about my trouble with
    reading?
Did Pa tell the Oblingers my schooling's
    done,
or did she think a girl my age
who's not in school
mustn't be able to learn?

*"The girl's not fit for learning,"*
Teacher whispered,
but not quietly enough.
I overheard her
telling the superintendent
during his visit,

*"She'll know answers,
but she don't read right."*

*Not fit,*
what Mrs. Oblinger
thinks of me too.

"I'll be leaving early,"
Mr. Oblinger tells us at supper.
"I've got plenty to do in town.
Anything you need?"

"Bring letters!" Mrs. Oblinger pleads.
He touches her cheek.
"I'll see what's at the post office."

After supper Mr. Oblinger pulls me aside.
"You might have noticed
my wife's missing home.
Keep her company tomorrow while I'm away."

I'd rather muck out a barn
barefoot.

"Yes, sir."

It's wet when Mr. Oblinger leaves.
Already there are patches
where the muslin ceiling drips.
I have cleared the breakfast table
and washed up.
There is nothing more to keep me busy.

Mrs. Oblinger sits in her rocker,
lights a candle to bring sense to the dark.
I wonder if the same summer storm
keeps Hiram and Pa inside.

I sit down at the table,
start to mend a shirt.

"I was wrong in trying this,"
Mrs. Oblinger says,
"but his letter was so kind.
I didn't think through prairie living."

She rocks.
"If my brother hadn't shown him my
    photograph,
I wouldn't be stuck here."
I fiddle with a button and thread.

She stops the chair.
Her voice is louder:
"I'm not one of those mail-order brides,
if that's what you're thinking."

I lift my eyes from my sewing.
"No, ma'am," I say.

She rocks again.
"The quiet out here's the worst part,
thunderous as a storm the way
it hounds you
inside
outside
nighttime
day."

I shift to miss a leaking patch forming
    overhead,
hoping she doesn't expect me to talk.
Because what can I say?
The prairie's hard on some,
but it's home to me,
and Mr. Oblinger has tried.

"I hate this place," she whispers.

Before I think better, I say,
"He's left a shade tree out front,
he's plastered the walls,
and he's putting in a proper floor."

"What'd you say?"

Does she even remember I'm here?

"Mr. Oblinger's a good man," I try again.
"He wants to make this home for you."

She stands over me now.
"You think plaster makes a difference in this
    place?
Look at this."
She holds out her mud-caked skirt.
"It's filthy in here!
The ceiling leaks.
Sometimes snakes get through!"

The cool sod's where they like to nest.
"They help with mice," I offer.

She glares.

I want to know how old she is.
(Four years,
maybe five
ahead of me?)
I want her to know
she'll learn to make a home.

"When it's wet outside
and our roof leaks,
Ma and I crawl under the table
and wait for the storm to pass."

She glares again,
but slowly lowers herself to the dry earth.
I settle next to her.

Under the table
we sit,
arms wrapped around our knees,
while water puddles on the bench.
It's possible for a soddy roof to collapse.
I stick my head out.
More soil has gathered in fabric folds,
but the ceiling looks like it will hold.

"Getting hungry?" I ask.
Mrs. Oblinger nods.
I fetch a pot with last night's beans
and hand her a spoon.
We eat in silence,
listening for the wagon and a change
   in the rain.

The even rhythm of the rain lessens.
I pull open the door and step outside.
It's good to feel the open space.

At the creek
the water rushes
where before it was calm.

The missus won't talk to me.
I'm the one who fed her,
thought to bring the quilt
to the only dry spot.
She lies under the table
with her boots on.

I take the linens
and hang them on the line.

Ma's got
her quilts drying.
Hiram's out
to milk the cow.
Pa's turning soil,
grateful for the rainfall.

I'm miles away.

Thank goodness Mr. Oblinger
built this house on a slope.
There is no water at the door.
With it open,
a bit of air
might help to dry the muddy floor
before night comes.

＊

I sleep in the rocker,
the driest spot
besides the makeshift bed,
where Mrs. Oblinger rests.

＊

The coffee's on;
still she doesn't stir.
The creek runs smoothly now.
He should be home soon.

I hear the wagon
and head outside.
It's best if Mr. Oblinger sees me first.

He swings down from the seat.
"How'd you fare?"
"The missus is tired," I say,
unsure of how to explain
why she's not yet left her place
under the table.

She's up now,
sitting at the table.
He's given her the coffee,
thick from waiting on the stove.

She holds a letter,
stares at it for a time,
folds it,
stands,
pushes past the doorway
into sun and open prairie.

Was it real,
that talk we had
the rainy day Mr. Oblinger was in town?
She rarely speaks,
and if she does it's to criticize.
Does she think I like it here?
She's not the only one
missing family,
wishing for familiar voices.
She chose this place.

Can't Mr. Oblinger see
the slow pulling away,
the distance
growing
in this tiny space?
When she sits around back,
I imagine she's counting the miles
between here and home.

Mr. Oblinger and Mr. Chapman
split logs,
lay planks.
I bring out the pail and dipper
and offer them a drink.
Mr. Chapman nods his thanks.
His beard's fuller than Mr. Oblinger's,
but his clothes nonetheless look like town.
Seems like all the folks west of home are new.
Even so,
Pa would approve of their labors.
"Many hands make light work," he'd say.

They labor until the furniture is restored to its
    rightful place.
There is only the entryway to complete.

The men shake hands.
"Much obliged," Mr. Oblinger says.
Mr. Chapman shrugs.
"It's what neighbors do.
I'd appreciate if you could check in on my
    place
once or twice.
I'm going east for a visit,
may not be back before the first snow."

A fine breeze stirs,
the sunflowers nod,
the day she chooses to go riding.
Usually she stays close,
like a tethered calf.

"Pack some biscuits, will you, May?
I want to see all that I can.
The prairie's so beautiful today."
She's never spoken that way before.
"Tell my husband I'll be a while.
Don't count on me for dinner."

When Mr. Oblinger hears,
he smiles.
"It's good to see her happy.
Maybe I'll be done with this floor
before she's back."

I stop Mr. Oblinger as he works
to remind him to eat.
My day's quiet;
I mend
and iron.
I work numbers
and look at a passage in my reader,
the one Hiram helped me with,
about the vastness of the ocean,
the limitlessness of the sea.
His voice in my head helps me when
    I stumble.

I've never seen water spread
straight to the horizon;
these endless grasslands
are sea enough for me.
This soddy's like an island
far from any shoreline.
My home is out there
somewhere.
To me,
a world away.

Maybe because the day is different,
it takes me time to notice
the note　　　.
left on the bedside crate,
where she always kept her Bible.

*Mr. Oblinger,*
*You've been so kind,*
*but I can't stay.*
*I'm taking the train*
*back to Ohio.*
*Please understand.*
*Louise*

I whisper the words,
go through the letter several times,
and I understand.

Mrs. Oblinger's gone.

The biscuits.
She planned to make this look like a simple
　　ride,
but she prepared ahead of time.

Mr. Oblinger works;
the floor is almost done,
for her.

I hand him the message.
"The missus left this."

He walks outside to read in the light.
I pull farther back in.
This is his business,
not mine.

# 4

I busy my hands with sweeping
the almost-finished floor.

"I need to get to town," he says.
"She probably don't remember the way."
He reaches for his hat
and in his haste
almost trips over the scattered wood.

"Don't worry about supper,"
he says.
"I could be gone some time."

He hitches the other horse to the wagon,
lays his rifle across his knees,
and drives,
fast as lightning sparks fire,
quick as flames consume the prairie.

Even at home,
if Pa and Ma drive into town,
I've got Hiram for company.
And there's Bessie in the barn and the
    laying hens.
Here,
there is no cow yet,
no chickens roosting.
I watch the wagon
until I see nothing on the open plain.
For the first time ever,
I am alone.

Fear flashes inside me.
Pa never left Hiram and me without
    protection.
All around me there is nothing
but the prairie and the sky.
"Silly girl," I tell myself.
"There's no reason to worry."
But it takes a time for my heart to slow.

I stretch out on the grass;
sweet sunshine warms my face.
I stay like this all afternoon.
My chores can wait.

I wake
to evening shadow,
confused.
The wagon is still gone.

Inside I pick an apple from the barrel,
light a candle,
work numbers on my slate.

When I sit up,
my slate falls to the floor.
The candle's burned out.
Morning light filters through the papered
    window.
The other bed is empty.

The missus must have made it far
if they stayed in town overnight.

I have to fetch the water,
gather fuel for the stove.
Some string beans might be ready to pick.

They'll need a good meal
when they return.

## 45

I weed the garden
and watch toward town.
Nothing moves against the horizon.

For a time I sit on my heels,
the soddy at my back,
the open prairie before me,
waiting.

There is still no sign of the Oblingers
by the time I've reached the last garden row.
I stand and wipe the dirt
from the front of my dress.

Surely
they'll be back
for supper.

The beans have cooked so long
they are like lumpy corn mush.
I sit in the rocker
with the door open wide.

Maybe something has happened to them.

❋

I dread the blackness
growing stronger outside.

In bed
I hear
the sounds
I miss
when
others
sleep nearby.

The breeze
rattles
at the papered window
and pushes
at the door.

Burrowed
in the quilt,
I hug my knees,
try
not
to listen.

I know there's
something
moving
near the stove.

A mouse,
not
a footstep,
I tell myself.
I would have heard
the wagon
and the welcome sound
of voices.

Gooseflesh ripples
up my arms.
I squeeze my knees tighter.
When
will morning
come?

Maybe Mrs. Oblinger
lost her way,
and her husband never found her.
He could be riding from home to home,
asking after her.

Maybe she rode past town.
Maybe the horse broke its leg.
What if Mr. Oblinger is tired of her?
He might have let her take the train,
and now he's in town,
biding his time.

If Pa knew Mr. Oblinger
had up and left,
he'd rush over to get me,
and when he saw the Oblingers,
he'd give them a tongue-lashing,
for sure.

But Pa
doesn't know,
and I
don't know
what has happened.

What will happen.
Whether I should be
mad,
or scared,
or whether I should prepare a meal:
their welcome supper.

On the fourth day,
I stand at the stove
and, with my finger on the calendar,
trace the days of August.

I've known it since last night:
it's been too long to expect them
to return.

Something's happened.

My legs fold under me
as I try
to catch
my breath
between sobs.

Why would Mr. Oblinger
leave me alone?
Why would that woman
run away?
Why must I be stuck
twice
where I don't want to be,
with no way to tell
Pa, Ma, Hiram,
with
no one
to care for me?

I push open the door
and run,
and run,
and run,
and run,
until the soddy's a tiny speck.
And around me,
the grass reaches in every direction.
There is nothing here to mark my place,
nothing to show me where I am.
No trees.
No stones.
No wagon ruts this way.
Just emptiness.
This isn't home,
where I know the land.

I turn back,
running,
until my surroundings are familiar,
the soddy's larger on the horizon.
I must stay close,
so as to not lose my way.

When the sun is low
and my tears have dried,
I stir from my spot in the grass.
I open the door to the Oblingers' home.
The sudden dark,
cool space
is quiet,
empty,
and strange.

Pa doesn't know they won't return.
The nearest neighbor is gone.

I'm here till Christmas.

# Part Two

# 53

So many times I've wished for just a minute
to linger
before beginning chores,
or wished I could skip
the washing up after supper—
Now I can do what I want.

No one's going to tell me
to gather fuel
or start the biscuits.
There's no need to cook.
I've got a barrel of apples,
a bit of corn bread left
from yesterday.
I can light the lamp.
No one can tell me I'm being wasteful,
using the light just for schoolwork,
or that it's time for bed.

I can do what I want.

My reader and slate
don't need to be hidden away.
I can keep them out with me.

With an apple in hand,
I open my reader:

*I have been infromed—*

*I have been informed that stranger the name
Goodman . . .*

The letters aren't working.

*. . . have been informed that a stranger name
Goodman . . .*

I can't place the words where they belong.

*. . . the name of Goodman has settled near you
hope you find in agreeable . . .*

I squeeze my eyes shut,
try to focus.

*. . . hope you find him in agreeable . . .*

Do it again, May.

*. . . find him an . . . find in him an-a*
*greeble . . .*

My fingernails dig into the cover

*. . . ana greeable . . .*

I fling my reader;
it smacks the wall.

Why can't I do this?
What is
wrong
with me?
I can speak,
and hear,
and see,
and understand when someone reads to me.

I follow lessons at school,
and Ma's directions in the kitchen.
I know what words mean.

So why can't I do this?

I
must
be
stupid.

## 54

It is morning.
There is no water,
no fuel.
It was foolish to waste time last night.

A sack of buffalo chips
next to the stove,
water from the stream,
coffee in the pot;
I cannot
let
myself
think.
Just do chores, May.
Keep moving,
go pick some corn.
Maybe I could try to finish the floor
Mr. Oblinger left undone.
There are only a few boards missing.

I bang at the boards,
not sure exactly
where to place each piece,
but figuring with so few to go,
the planks will show me where they belong.

Maybe Mr. Oblinger will
want to fix these boards
to his liking
someday.
I stop myself.

He's never coming back.

I am afraid
in the dark
all alone
I am afraid

It started small:
Hiram's church-going shirt left untucked,
My dirty hands at suppertime.
Then we got bold:
Sneaked a piece of cooling pie,
waded deeper in the stream
than Pa allowed.

Somehow Hiram rarely caught trouble.
That smile of his softened Ma.
Pa, grateful for extra hands,
overlooked the times Hiram forgot to milk,
misplaced the saw,
dropped his boot in the creek.

I thought of something he wouldn't dare do.
"Get Ma's scissors
and meet me out back."

It was just the two of us behind the soddy,
but I leaned in close.
"Cut some of my hair."

He narrowed his eyes.
"Why'd I want to do that?"

"Afraid Ma will notice?" I sang.
"Worried Pa will tell you
to wait for him in the barn?"

"You're daring me?" he asked.

"I am," I said.

That was enough to stir him.
And when he grabbed at a braid
and the scissors snapped,
I scooped it up,
a four-inch rope of brown hair.
Swishing it under his nose, I told him,
"You're going to get it tonight."

That smile of his lit up his face.
"Don't I know it."

I swatted at him with the braid,
yelled, "I'm showing Ma!"
and ran.

It is not strange
to wear the same dress
from day to day,
but to awake,
still clothed,
and not notice
until the coffee's made—

I hope Mrs. Oblinger fell off that horse
and is still wandering the prairie.
Mr. Oblinger
better be dead.

Pa deserves the mess he's made,
sending me here.
His only daughter
abandoned
by strangers,
forgotten
by family,
left behind
by classmates,
ignored
by Teacher.

Nobody cares
about me.

I hate this place.

Today,
if it takes forever,
I will see the place
where the earth touches sky.
I will find it.
I will track it down.
I will not sit here and wait
for nobody to come,
for nothing to happen.
Have Hiram and I been wasting time
on a foolish game?
Today,
I will learn the truth.

✳

Over my shoulder I check for the soddy
one time,
two times,
three.
Why did I think I'd be brave enough
to set out on my own?

How did Hiram and I
get this idea anyway?

The earth is round,
Miss Sanders told us.
She brought that globe to school,
let us pass it around.

If stories were true,
I'd follow a bread-crumb path
all the way home.

But I have no heart for fairy tales
anymore.

I return to the soddy,
gather pebbles at the creek,
and line them up,
a family of smooth stones.
One by one
I heave them into the water,
harder,
then harder still,
until I'm wet,
and hoarse from yelling,
and done with childish dreams.

I have decided
there is no need to iron
my dresses
or the linens.
And my hair,
I don't have to pull it back
in a braid.
My coffee
doesn't need to be hot.

Who will notice?

I think it might be September,
if I've counted right.

Some days I sit at the creek,
the sun on my back,
collecting pill bugs
from under rocks.
They curl into a ball at the slightest touch,
then,
waiting,
unfold themselves to continue their journey,
this time on my wrist,
my thumb,
the frayed cuff of my dress.

I hold them,
watch them rush,
wonder
what sort of task could hurry
such a creature along.

I lie in the sunshine,
thankful
for the freshness of the grass,
the babbling company of the stream.

Some days I sit in the rocker,
the quilt about me though it's hot outside.
I shun the sunlight,
groan to think of the water I must fetch,
the steps I'll have to take,
the work that's needed
just to exist.

Wouldn't it be better
to
forget
to
care?

Wouldn't it be easier
to stay in the hazy place where dreams come,
to simply fade away?

I crouch under the table,
listening
to the rain
drip on the supper dishes I left out
in my rush
to stay dry.

My thoughts drift back to Teacher.
I can't let them happen
here,
under the table,
where there's no task to keep me busy.

The bedding is wet.
I try to find a way to sleep
that allows for comfort,
but I can't.
My memories catch up with me.
I wonder what Teacher had to say
when I didn't return to school?

*"The girl's finally got some sense,
staying home."*

Maybe I was only smart before Teacher came.

*It's because you won't try.*

Teacher,
I've tried more than you will ever know,
out in the barn,
with my book,
and my voice
shaking.

The words on paper
don't match the sounds I make.
I have to memorize
to even try to read aloud.

So
if you think I can't read,
Teacher,
then maybe you're right.

Coffee,
a half sack of dried beans,
flour, sugar, and cornmeal.
The sugar's not good for much
when eating simple things.
But the flour—
with my bit of sourdough starter—
keeps providing for biscuits
like I used to bake
with Ma.

The last of the meat ran out long ago.

A tin of peaches
is all that is left
of Mrs. Oblinger's fine things.
I've told myself I must hold out longer
before I touch them.
They're stashed,
like a promise,
behind the rest.

I pull the door open,
stand with my hands on my hips,
and yell into the morning:
"Guess what, Mrs. Oblinger?
I don't think you're too bright
yourself!"

What does it matter if she can't hear me?
If it was long ago
she called me stupid?

"Hope you enjoyed your ride
on that lovely prairie day!"

I lift my dusty skirts,
sashay like someone fancy,
curtsy to the cabbage,
think on the missus and her eastern ways:
good riddance.

I have almost eaten
to the bottom of the apple barrel.

When the world is black,
I'm most alone,
the silence thick around me.
I pray for wind,
for rain,
for the meadowlark
to break
the constant pound of quiet.

What is that?
What is at the door?

A rasping sound,
a muffled breath,
a whine
outside.
Then, nothing.

My pulse surges through my fingertips
as I crack open the door.
Scratches line the heavy wood,
yellow threads cut deeply in the boards.

There are tracks
on the edge of the moonlit garden.

A wolf has been here.
I am not alone.

Avery Pritchard told me
that when his pa's away
at night,
sometimes a pack of wolves surrounds their
    soddy.
The wolves sense a difference about the place.
They howl,
they scratch,
but mostly,
they sit and wait.
Can they smell that someone's missing?
Do they sense the fear inside?

Mrs. Pritchard tells the children stories,
presses her forehead against the windowpane,
and says, "Get on, you!"

Last spring,
in the early dawn,
Mrs. Pritchard took the shotgun
and waited by the door.
When she heard the wolf pack stirring,
she aimed and fired.
The pack rolled off like summer storm clouds.
One skinny female lay dead.

Avery's ma dragged that wolf to the door
and left it,
a hairy mound,
at the entrance to their soddy.
All day she stepped over it
when she went to milk
or fetch water.
She wouldn't let anyone else outside.

When Mr. Pritchard arrived,
she didn't say a word,
just handed him the shovel
and shut the door.

Avery's pa buried the wolf out back.

Now,
when he has business in town,
he makes sure to hurry home
come nightfall.

Mr. Oblinger
took the rifle.

When Miss Sanders came
to teach our school,
she was the first to understand
I could get the words
from the book
to my mind
more easily if I listened to lessons.

She didn't force me to read
in front of everyone.

Once she brought me
a book about a boy named Tom Sawyer
because she thought I'd find Tom like Hiram.
She read it during recess
just for me.

But when Miss Sanders married,
she left our school
and Teacher came.

The garden has given up
its last yield.
Some withered string beans,
a dozen potatoes,
five ears of corn,
one small head of cabbage,
crawling with bugs.

Days and nights run together.
Sometimes I forget how
I got to this place
or why I am still here.

Maybe it is October?

There was frost
this morning,
but it melted quickly.

❈

There's no time left for waiting.
There is nothing holding me here.
I can't abide this place any longer.

I pack my pillowcase:
one extra dress wrapped around my worthless
    reader,
one stocking filled with corn bread,
one with biscuits.
On top of this,
two ears of corn
and a cup.

I button Ma's fine boots.
I wish I had insisted on keeping Hiram's old
    ones,
but I know Ma gave me hers
for herself as much as me,
a message to Mrs. Oblinger,
fresh from the city,
showing that women out here still have some
    grace.
My feet will hurt, I reckon,
before I make it far.

The broom's my only weapon.
I think on Ma,
the way she swatted Hiram when he snatched
    the bacon.

I grasp the handle,
throw my pillowcase over one shoulder,
and step out onto the prairie.

How did Pa get here?
I see nothing to point the way.
I walk alongside the Oblingers' little creek,
hoping it will lead to the river,
to a neighbor,
to the outskirts of town.

The grass has dried to silver-green;
it slaps my legs as I push forward.
Sweat trickles between my shoulder blades.
Impossible to think there was frost just
    this morning.

I have only the stream
and endless grasses to guide me.

Sometimes I see wagon ruts,
a memory pressed in dried mud.
If western Kansas had more folks,
this would be easier.
There might be a well-worn path by now.

Grasshoppers whir,
fly about me.
I swat at them with the broom.

My stomach clenches,
so I shake some crumbled corn bread from
   the stocking
straight into my mouth.
Then up ahead,
I spot the jagged branches of a currant bush.
Late-summer birds have picked over
the berries that remain.
I grab at what's left,
red-black juice staining my fingers,
eating,
eating,
pocketing the dry ones,
squatting until my knees ache.

I stand and stretch,
look behind me,
recognizing nothing.
Something rustles,
and I reach for the broom.
Like me,
the animal freezes.
We stay that way
until my shoulders throb.

Then
a jackrabbit leaps beside me.
I drop the broom,
fall back,
glimpse it dashing zigzag.

My breath comes short
and painful.
"It was a rabbit," I say,
but the words mean nothing
to the weakness creeping up my legs.

Here's what's true:
Already
the evening sky is pushing back the daylight.

Gooseflesh tingles on my arms.
I don't know where I am,
I can't know where I'm going.

And suddenly,
I'm running
back!
I'm running—
my heels slam into the hard-packed earth.
Running—
my breath's jagged.
Running—
birds scatter from their grass nests.
I need those walls around me!
The pillowcase slaps my back.

Pain rips through my ankle.
I tumble to the ground
and curse the hole I've stepped in.

The sky is almost black when,
limping,
I reach the soddy.

## 83

My ankle's purple.
Those stupid boots.

Fetching water today,
I catch a glimpse of myself in the stream:
hair hanging in clumps,
dress ripped at one shoulder.
I haven't used the washtub since
the Oblingers left.
My eyes study the dirty girl.

I finger the last few currants
still in my pocket.
Maybe I could go back and check for more.
If I hadn't been startled,
if I'd stuck it out a little longer,
I'd have bulging apron pockets.
Maybe I'd have reached another soddy.
That neighbor Mr. Chapman's gone,
but if I'd found his place,
surely he'd have some jerky,
a tin of soda crackers left behind.

But now,
with this ankle,
I can't go far.
And the wolf.
I shiver,
remembering how frightened I was
of just a little rabbit.

I sit beside the stream
dipping my fingers in the icy water.
In summer,
Pa and Hiram bring in trout,
speckled bodies writhing

in their hands.
I trail my fingers,
wiggling them like Hiram showed me.
Nothing happens.

I run,
holding my skirts above my knees.
I holler
and skip
and make faces at the outhouse.
I slam the door,
take a spoon to the pots and pans.

I whistle,
I spit,
think up as many unladylike things as I can,
and do them.

Out in the open.
For the whole empty world to see.

A thin sheet of ice crept across
the water pail last night.
I take the dipper and push through
to scoop a drink,
then stir the fire
for breakfast.

❋

The sky
holds the high white
of snow.
It is too early
for this.
I am not ready.

Maybe there won't be a storm
after all.
Autumn is devious.
Calm afternoons with no hint of breaking
can turn violent,
bringing wind,
ushering in rain
and even snow.

Or maybe I haven't been paying enough
attention
and I'll get trapped out here
in
a
blizzard.

On
my
own.

*Maybe May B.*
*Maybe*

Snow is falling.
Why did I not prepare
when the weather first turned?
I have left
so many things
undone.
Maybe I should check the garden
for one last potato.
I should have gathered more chips to burn
yesterday.

Wind runs across the prairie,
swirling snowflakes and brittle grass.
I push through the icy gale,
force open the barn door.

Only one bale of hay is still intact.
I squat to lift it,
hardly seeing where I'm going,
and make it to the soddy more by memory
than sight.
My sore ankle complains.

Back in the barn,
I kneel in the scattered hay,
scooping armfuls into my dress,
and press the hem against my waist.
Outside again,
the blinding white whips at my eyes.
I bend my head for some protection.
Snow gathers at the soddy door.
I shove it open with a shoulder,
dump the hay,
and turn toward the barn
again and again,
until what hasn't blown away

is scattered
across the puncheon floor.

Once,
after weeks of rain,
Pa had Hiram and me
twist hay
into bundles for burning.

Now I sit in almost-darkness,
binding hay in logs
that won't flame out,
as just a handful would.

Stepping over
piles of hay bundles,
bits of loose grass,
I reach into the barrel

for the last apple.

For a moment I think
I've left the lamp burning,
but the brightness isn't
exactly the same.
Around me,
it's as clear as midday,
The papered window alight.

I slip out of bed.
Bits of hay stick to my feet
as I pull open the door.
A thin layer of snow blankets the entrance,
sparkling in the morning sun.

❀

If only
I'd not panicked that day
I tried to go.
But with the snow,
it's too late to consider again.

Whether or not I want to be here,
I am.

The sun is out.
Ma's boots leave
soft gray marks
in the melting snow.
It is too early for
winter to last.

I will be ready next time.

My arm pricks as I lower it into the stream;
the water's even colder than before.
I press my body to the bank,
trying to cast no shadow,
reaching deeper with my hand.

Why did I never try for fish with Pa
    and Hiram?

Soon I can hardly feel
my wiggling fingers,
but I keep moving,
hoping trout will notice.

Something flits below the surface,
curves gracefully,
slips by.
I watch for movement farther upstream
and let my fingers dance
like moss,
like water bugs,
like tadpoles beating tiny tails.

Then I spy one!
It's smooth,

a ribbon of color
running
down its middle.

My fingers wave;
it approaches.
I am close enough to stroke its belly,
and with one quick jerk,
I grab that fish and throw it on the bank.

Three fish—
My stomach's full
for the first time in weeks.

I've thought through arithmetic
and worked some problems on my slate.
I've recited states
alphabetically
and
in the order of their joining the Union.

My reading I've avoided
ever since that day
nothing worked right.

Lamplight shines on my book,
its blue cover frayed at the corners,
the spine a lighter shade
in the middle
where my hand grips,
finger smudges on the back.

I examine it like it's the first time
Ma handed it to me,
the reader she brought
all the way to Kansas.

She didn't know then,
I didn't know,

the tricks words would play
on me.

What if I were to pretend
the struggles never happened?
What if I were to open this book,
go back,
start
fresh?

My fingers feel almost as chilled as they did
this afternoon
under the water,
but didn't I pull three fish to the surface?
Didn't I gut them,
cook them up,
and eat my fill?

Surely
these words
can't be as difficult
to grasp,
as slippery to work with.

I find the page that tripped me weeks ago,

press along the spine.

I shut my eyes,
breathe deeply,
tell myself nothing will change
or surprise me
when I open my eyes.

No one is listening.

*I have need—*

No.

*I have been in formed that a stragner . . .*
*a stranger*
*named Goodman . . .*

Slowly, May,
don't go on what you remember.
The words begin to swim,
but I hold fast.
Just one sentence to push through.

*. . . have been informed that a stranger*

*of the name of Goodman has settled near you.*

I press the cover closed with both hands.
My heart thrums
as I turn down the lamp,
slip into bed,
filled to bursting.

From the calendar I tear away
one month,
then two.
Is it October
or November?

Time was made
for others,
not for someone
all alone.

The fish rest deeper now.
I cook beans day after day.
Sometimes I bake corn bread,
but the meal's getting low.

If I eat just a little,
there will be food for weeks to come.
My mind knows this,
but my fingers shake with every bite,
and I've taken to checking my rations
over and over,
licking my finger,
sweeping it under the cornmeal sack,
hoping for a few more grains.

The tin of peaches,
still tucked behind the sugar,
I won't open until I must.

I pull it down from the shelf,
hold it in my hand.
"Peaches," I read aloud.
"Fresh picked."
My voice sounds funny,
like that odd instrument

Mr. Wolcott brought to the literary social
   last year.
He pulled and squeezed
the black thing;
it opened like a folded piece of cloth.
Accordion,
I think he called it.
"Peaches.
Fresh picked," I say again.

I move my finger under each word:
"Peaches.
Fresh picked!"

Ma would be horrified,
but Ma's not here to see
I've slept most of the morning away.
It would be nice
to lounge and doze
as long as I feel like staying abed,
but it's more burden than comfort
because of all the time to remember:

When Teacher came,
I hoped she would be
like Miss Sanders,
but I should have known
from the start:
Teacher
wasn't the same.

"I want to see what each of
you is capable of," Teacher announced,
even before she sat down.
"Youngest ones first.
We'll work our way to the top of the school."
With a ruler she pointed to the first row.
"Stand and recite the alphabet."

Jemmy Thompson's lip
turned down,
the way a newborn's
does before it starts wailing,
but he managed to make it through.

"Older grades."
Teacher eyed us in the back.
Rita Howard had to start over three times,
her voice too soft
for Teacher's liking.
Teacher scolded Hiram for rushing
through his piece.

And then it was my turn.
I opened to "The Voice of the Wind."
With Hiram's help,
I'd read it through just the night before.

Did Teacher sense
what everyone thought
as I walked—
knees like water—
to the front of the room?
Their thoughts weren't audible,

but I heard them just the same.

I took a deep breath.
Maybe this time I could do it.
Maybe Teacher would never have to know.

I held my reader in front of me,
high enough so I wouldn't have to see
    their faces,
both elbows squeezed to my sides.

>   *"I am the when.*
>   *Wind.*
>   *I am wind and I . . ."*

Rita covered her mouth
with her prissy little fingers.

>   *". . . I am the wind and I—"*

Teacher rapped the ruler on her desk.
"Excuse me, child.
What is your name?"

Warm tears splashed my feet.

Something was broken inside.
My new teacher knew.

Just like my reading,
my words were slow to form.
"May-vis, ma'am."

"Well, May-vis," she said,
like my name tasted sour,
"I think you're sitting in the wrong part
of the schoolroom.
Kindly move to the second row."

"Ma'am?"
I turned my head just a little,
not wanting to show my tears.
She was seating me with the little ones?

"I said"—
she spoke louder now,
like I was hard of hearing—
"move to the front of the room."

I glanced at Hiram.
He shrugged,

but his eyes hardly met mine.
I fetched my slate
and slid in next to Jemmy,
whose feet didn't yet meet the floor.

It's the noise that wakes me
in the darkness close as a shroud.
Wind whips about the soddy;
I imagine I hear the walls groan.

Prairie quiet
is rarely silent.

Mrs. Oblinger called it
lonely wailing;
it made her fret and talk of home.

I feel my way across the room.
Just cracking the door open
drives fresh snow over my feet.

For all Mrs. Oblinger's fussing,
she'd never seen what the worst prairie
    winds bring,
what is coming—
I wipe at tears I haven't noticed until now.

Blizzard.

Stumbling toward the stove,
I reach for my jar of starter.
It can't freeze;
I'll need biscuits.

In bed I huddle in a ball,
two quilts about me,
the starter jar against my chest.

The first time I heard the chant
was the recess after Teacher moved me
to the front
with the babies
missing their ma,
still losing their milk teeth,
swinging their legs when Teacher
    looked away.

When Teacher dismissed us from lessons,
I met Hiram at the farthest edge of the
    schoolyard.
"I don't think you need to worry none.
She'll figure out you're smart real soon.
May Betts, don't let her get to you."
He had that look that reminds me
someday he'll be a man.

Behind us I thought
I heard my name.

*May B.*
*May B.*

I turned around,

but no one was calling.

"Let's go play."
Hiram gave me a shove.

We picked sides pretty quick
until it got to me.
Rita whined to Avery,
"Maybe May will freeze in the middle of
    the game,
just like she did this morning."

"May B. can play just fine,"
Nathaniel said, tossing the ball in the air.
"Keep the picks going."

"Maybe she can, maybe she can't."
Rita stared straight at me.

Some of the little ones started up:
"Maybe she can, maybe she can't. . . ."

Avery said,
"May's good and you know it."
He beckoned to me.

"Come join us."
Rita scowled.

"Maybe she can, maybe she can't,
Maybe she can, maybe she can't. . . ."

I turned away,
the taunt following me to the schoolhouse.

## 102

The air is still
when I awake.
I remember immediately:
blizzard.

The door won't budge
with the first tug
or the second.

I press my foot against the wall,
yank one last time.
A barrier of blue-white snow
stands solid.

Slamming the door,
I spin around,
press my back against it.
There is so little space
to live in,
to draw in air,
to move.
The walls hold everything so close.

I need to get out!

Swinging the door open again,
I dig like a prairie dog.

When Hiram and I had snowball fights,
I hated the feel
of snow trapped at my wrists
between mittens and coat.
Now it slips down my sleeves,
gathers in the elbows of my dress,
and I don't pay it any mind.
I have to get out of here.

I dig until my fingers throb.
I dip them in the pail,
and the icy water
burns like liquid fire.
But slowly I am able to move my hands.

Looking over my shoulder,
I see the mound
heaped on the floor
and the useless hole
I've dug.

I clench the pail in my reddened hands

bent like claws
and throw it at the hole.
Water splatters everything—
the table,
yesterday's beans,
even the twisted hay in the basket
and the precious few buffalo chips.
How could I have done something so
    thoughtless?

*"Stupid girl."*
If Mrs. Oblinger could see me now.

*"The girl's not right,"*
Teacher would say.
*"Something don't work proper in her head."*

I grip my reader,
open it to the middle,
rip a handful of paper from the spine.
My numb hands fumble at the stove
    door latch.
I tug it open
and watch the pages burn.

"This is what a Maybe gets!"
I shout.

Sobbing,
I sink to the floor;
the rough wood scrapes my knees
as I crawl back to bed
and bury myself under the quilts.

## 103

"I won't," I told Teacher.

She lifted my chin with a finger.
"You won't or you can't?"

I felt my cheeks flame
there in front of everyone,
all those eyes
examining me like an oddity,
some abnormal thing.

"I won't," I said again.

She thrust the book before me,
the copy Miss Sanders had left behind.
"Read it," she said.

Hiram's lips moved,
saying something I couldn't follow.
Everyone waited,
staring at me.
My insides clenched.

It was the chapter where Tom returns,
witnesses his own funeral.

So many complicated words
too easy to trip on.
I kept my mouth closed,
tried to keep my breathing calm.

Teacher's voice got higher. "Well?"

She stood there,
waiting to pounce at my first mistake.
Wanting to make a fool of me,
ready to show how stupid I was.

"I won't!" I shouted at her.

She gripped my wrist
and I was thankful
for the pain,
thankful
for an excuse
to cry.

"Then kindly find your way home.
Only come back when you're ready to learn."

What if I'd read that first paragraph perfectly?

She'd have argued I'd had Hiram whisper
   answers.

She never believed I could,
anyhow.

I am going to stay here,
wrapped in these quilts,
let the fire die,
and freeze to death
or maybe starve,
whichever comes first.
Then Pa will be sorry
for sending me here.
Was it worth
those few dollars
to find
your daughter dead?

I peek out of the quilts
at the snow mound on the floor.
The cold pinches at my nose.
The stove spits out so little warmth,
I choose to stay abed,
freezing,
rather than risk the chill in moving
from bed to fire.

It was a good reading day,
that afternoon I asked Miss Sanders.
We'd worked all recess together,
my voice sure and strong.

She'd always told me she believed in me,
that I could make the reading happen,
to give it time
and practice.
Now she sat at her desk,
preparing for our after-recess lesson.

"Do you think I could earn a teaching
    certificate
once I'm old enough?"

Miss Sanders,
always brimming with kindness,
fiddled at her desk far too long.

"I'm sorry, May, what was that?"
But
her face said,
Please don't ask me again,
don't make me tell you something
that will only bring you hurt.

"It's nothing," I said,
and forced a smile.
"It's time for lessons.
I'll go ring the bell."

So many things
I know about myself
I've learned from others.
Without someone else to listen,
to judge,
to tell me what to do,
and to choose
who I am,
do I get to decide for myself?

Have I slept
or have I been awake all this time?
If Ma were here she'd say,
"May, get moving.
The day's not for resting."

With the quilts around me,
I shuffle across the floor
to the pot of leftover beans.
A layer of ice has formed
over them.
I don't care.
I crack it with a spoon
and hunch,
shivering,
swallowing without tasting at all.

I squeeze a hay log,
to feel if the cold
is ice
or just the air.
Only two logs don't crackle
the way the popcorn
in the skillet does.
The fire has burned so low,

I have to push it along,
stirring and blowing
before I place the hay logs
gently on the embers.
A lick of flame
grows brighter,
and I draw up close enough
to burn my eyebrows.

I am
Mavis Elizabeth Betterly.
I am
used to hard work.
I can
run a household better
than Mrs. Oblinger ever could.
What does it matter,
those things
that
hold me back?

What does it matter
when I make mistakes?
They don't
make me
who
I
am.

I search through Mrs. Oblinger's sewing box.
In front of her tiny looking glass,
I run my fingers through my hair,
then grip a handful
and cut.
The scissors snap
as sheaves fall loose upon the floor.

Samson didn't get to choose
what Delilah did,
tricking him into the haircut that sapped
   his strength.

I didn't ask
to read like a child,
quit school,
come here,
starve.

One last snip,
and the last strands
drop.
My hair is short.
Jagged.
I

made it this way,
not someone else.
I
chose
to hack it off.
This is of my own doing.

I grasp handfuls of hair,
Shove it
into the stove,
watch it
curl,
shrivel,
and burn.

It is time to figure out
how to care for myself,
not by waiting
or trying to forget I've been left here.
Living now,
not later on when Pa comes.
Not last year in my memory.

I bang ice from the hay logs.
The few buffalo chips must stay as they are,
too fragile to pound on the floor.
My hands move like wet leather
dried out in the sun.

I've taken to using my coat as another blanket;
my mittens I wear all the time;
I haven't removed Ma's boots for days.
Mr. Oblinger has clothing
stored beneath their bed,
and there's Mrs. Oblinger's trunk.
I'm not ready to root through
their underdrawers.
I will make do with what I have.

I study the soddy.

I've neglected to wash Mrs. Oblinger's pots.
Footprints cover the floor.
The bed's disheveled.

I straighten the cupboards
and find that can of peaches.

I place the tinned peaches on the table,
shake out the quilts,
folding them over the back of the rocker,
and sweep up the mess of dirt
on the floor.
With the broom I push snow into
  Mrs. Oblinger's pots,
to use later for washing.
The pail I fill also
and place near the stove.

I continue sweeping,
but can't push from my mind
stories I've heard:
people caught off guard in a blizzard
who wander,
looking for shelter,
lost for days
just yards from home.
The freezing starts in hands and feet,
then comes a sleep
with no waking.

I don't know what it is that reminds me
of the sourdough starter
still in the jar on the bed.
Surely it's frozen.
If I'd left it at the back of the stove,
the dough would still be
warm enough to work with.
I scoop up the jar.
The cold bites through my mittens,
but I must warm it myself.
The stove top would be too sudden.

I drag the rocker to the fire and sit,
climb into the quilts again,
and place the starter jar in my pillowcase,
doubling up the fabric.

Ma must be singing
"Old Dan Tucker" or "Home, Sweet Home"
right about now
as she boils potatoes.
Hiram's tooling leather,
maybe joining in the song:

*No more from that cottage again will I roam,*

*Be it ever so humble, there's no place like home.*

Pa's found a way out to the barn,
or if not,
he's working toward a way.

I imagine Ma and her broom
behind me
keeping time with the rocker.

I roll the starter jar
in my lap
the same way I scrub at laundry
on the washboard.
Back and forth,
my back hunched,
a tight pinch in my shoulders.


Sometimes Miss Sanders asked me to read
just to her.
The words would come more easily
without a full room watching.
Other times it would be just as difficult
as any other day.
She never lost patience
or said,
"We've been over this story again and again;
why can't you read it now?"
She'd say,
"Maybe tomorrow
the words will come right."
Or,
"Slower, May,
no need to rush. Take your time.
Let the words form

before you speak them."

Sometimes we would read together,
and those times my words were almost right,
her voice leading,
though still in step with mine.
I felt the rhythm of the words.
I heard the sounds needed to make them.
They didn't stick together or jumble on
    the page.

The starter is softer now.
I add it to the flour and roll out biscuits.

## 114

The calendar is tattered,
its corners curled and browned
from dirty hands
and moist prairie air.
I check to see where time might be,
though I stopped marking days
long ago.
For every month I'm sure I've spent at the
    Oblingers',
I subtract a week,
so as not to raise my hopes too high.

If Pa knew,
he'd be here,
faster than any train,
any buffalo stampede from the early
    prairie days,
faster than Hiram at school races,
to take me home.

I remove the pots from the stove,
letting the water cool just a bit,
then scrub at the crusted film left behind.
Mess slops on the floor;
wet patches bloom on the bodice of my dress.
I have no place to throw this filth,
no water to rinse clean.
For the first time since the blizzard morning,
I pull open the door,
dreading to see things left as they were before.

A shiny layer of ice on the solid wall of snow
reminds me of the water I threw.

With the broom handle,
I stab and pick
until I've made
a deeper hole.
I pour in the wash water.
The space stretches just a little.

I fill the pots with the snow I've scattered
and put them on the stove.

The snow muffles all noise,
so I am surprised when I hear the sound
    outside.
Scratching,
not the same as before,
that was dry claws
on dry boards.
Softer now,
like a rake dragged over freshly cut hay,
this scratching is persistent,
more urgent.

The wolf.

Can he smell the little food I have left?
But I know better.
He has no interest in corn bread and beans.
Wolves are carnivores.
They hunt rabbits, buffalo.
Pa's careful of an evening to bring Bessie to
    the barn.

Pain claws at my middle.
I know hunger too.

I'm as hollow as a washtub
turned over to dry.
I could make some biscuits,
or lick a handful of sugar,
but I reach for the peaches,
the last special treat
left by the Oblingers.

I trace my fingers over
*Fresh picked*
and say the words at the same time.

Sometimes with Miss Sanders,
I'd try different ways to read.
Once I held the rag she used
to wipe the blackboard.
When I struggled with a sound,
I'd squeeze the grimy cloth into a ball
and try again.
I don't know how,
but it helped the letters fall into place.

When Teacher came I'd focus so hard,
trying to imagine that balled-up rag.
I was ashamed

to stand with the little ones
in the front of the room.
I knew more than any of them,
more than Rita,
and Avery,
and Hiram,
put together.

Those days
I'd stumble some,
other times I'd make it through,
my fingernails leaving half-moons in my palm.

The peaches are cold,
smooth,
sweet.
I eat them with an ache in my stomach,
and swallow like Ma herself
spooned them up.

The buffalo chips are gone;
these hay twists must last.
No amount of modesty can keep me
from going through Mrs. Oblinger's trunk.

I pull at a corner of bright fabric
until it spreads across my lap.
The red dress.
Did Mrs. Oblinger make it back to Ohio?
I pull her dress over the three I already wear
and smooth it down,
remembering her soft hands,
oval fingernails,
never broken on a scrub board.
She hated me,
I think.
She thought I hated her.
Did I,
really?
Were we so very different?

I take a pair of Mr. Oblinger's stockings
and wear them over my mittens.

I wrap his muffler around my head,
burrow in the quilts and coat,
and rock before the stove.

Last night I dreamed Pa'd come
to get me.
He'd brought a shovel and dug,
scraping the snow
like a farmer breaking ground.

Again I rinse the pots.
The dishwater stretches
the opening in the snow wall
each time I pour it in.
The pots grow heavier
as I lift them.
What I wouldn't give for a bite of meat,
or that bug-infested cabbage.

I hope for a hint of light
reaching through the hole,
a reminder of the world outside.

Since the blizzard day,
I haven't opened my reader,
but now,
with a small scoop of beans
on the stove
and two biscuits from yesterday,
I sit in the rocker before the fire,
thankful for hot coffee,
and for the flicker of light
cast on the cover
of my book.

The pages fall open in my lap,
the spine empty in the center
where I ripped the paper out.
I flip back to see
which poems remain:
"Home and Its Memories,"
"The Battle of Hastings,"
"Light Out of Darkness."
I glance up at this last title,
taking in the shadows around me.
In this place,
I've met darkness like never before.
I understand light

because of these months
here.

I know this book,
remember what comes after each piece,
so that as I'm turning through,
I feel the space of missing pages getting
    nearer.
I know what shares the other side of "Light
    Out of Darkness."

Most of "The Voice of the Wind" is intact.
I run my finger under each word,
The ones that cost me my place at school,
that filled me with despair.

I know it by heart,
but I read it anyway,
trust my voice to lead me word by word:

> *I am*
> *the wind,*
> *and I*
> *blow,*
> *blow,*

*blow,*
*Driving*
*the rain*
*and the*
*beautiful*
*snow;*

I go slowly,
invite the words to find
a home
between
each breath.

No one is here
to listen,
or laugh.
I'm not whispering,
not mumbling,
I own this poem.

*Making confusion*
*wherever I go;*
*Roaring*
*and moaning,*
*Wailing and groaning.*

The words come faster.
Sometimes I twist them,
have to stop and try again.
But why should there be shame in that?
I'm doing it!
I'm reading!

> *Rounding the hill-top, I rush down the dale,*
> *Ruffling the river that waters the vale,*
> *Driving before me the white-winged sail.*

The first three stanzas remain,
the fourth left halfway:

> *'Cross desolate deserts I wildly roam;*
> *Wand'ring earth's corners, where nothing calls*
>     *home,*
> *I whisper in secret; I watch all alone,*

I know the rest I threw in the fire,
how the wind can lull,
can cheat and trick.
But today,
it's my turn to make my own ending.

# Part Three

I tuck a finger inside my reader
and reach for the basket of hay twists.

There are three left.

I need a plan.

I hold my bundled hands
against the stove door,
taking every last bit of heat
before I leave the rocker.

My feet are small enough
to wear three sets of stockings,
even if one boot doesn't button properly
over the ankle I twisted months ago.

I pocket the last two biscuits.
They will need to last me.

Pa's coming,
but I don't know when.

I shove the broom handle up
into the icy hole beyond the door
again
and again
until my shoulders burn.

Nothing changes.
Maybe if I took a spoon,
put it in the stove,
wrapped the handle in a bit of cloth,
I could
slowly
dig
my
way
out.

That wolf is somewhere out there.

I burn myself through cloth and stockings.
The spoon's heat is drawn almost instantly
once it touches snow.

What melts drips down my sleeves.
I return to the stove,
heat the spoon,
scrape,
scrape,
scrape,
until I've formed a hole deep enough
to try the broom handle again.
And though I thrust the handle with all
    I have left,
the snow ceiling still doesn't budge.

Maybe it is senseless digging out.
I am fifteen miles from home,
a distance a body could cover in one day
if nourished
and warm
and familiar with the way.
I might as well set out for the Pacific;
it's so big,
I reckon it would be easier to find.

My cropped hair falls across my face.
Senseless or not,
I will do what I have to,
what is right,
this moment,
for me.

How long do I heat the spoon,
pick at the snow,
swing the broom handle?
I'm shouting
like the wall will listen,
"Stupid blizzard. Danged ice!"
My hands blister beneath their layers.

The hole is big as my head.

How deep is this snow?

I've been so careful
not to waste the candles,
but that time is over now.

There are two left,
almost stubs.
I light one,
hold it in the snow hole.
Water drips
and the candle sputters out.
I light the second one and set it on the table,
then touch them wick to wick.
Every time the flame goes out,
I light my candle
and hold it to the snow again.

It is hard to tell what is sun,
what is candle,
what is pure hope.

The sound of the broomstick
against the snow
is less like a drum.
This is the soft thump
of kneading bread.

I swing the handle
faster and harder
with a power that has waited until now.

Suddenly
the broom handle sticks,
and I must yank it loose.
Snow tumbles down,
blessing me like
a downpour on parched fields.

The sky is blue!

I slip into my coat,
pack my pillowcase,
then straighten the soddy before I go.
If Mr. Oblinger does return someday,
I want him to find things in their proper
    places:
the bench tucked under the table,
the rocker angled properly.
There is nothing I can do with the dirty
    bean pot
except fill it with fresh snow.
I leave one quilt folded
over the back of the rocker.
The other will offer some protection outside.

I cling to the lower lip of the hole with one
    hand
and dig the toe of my boot into the snow wall,
heaving the quilt,
then the pillowcase
up and out,
and last of all,
the broom.

The sun is low in the east,
the sky is clear;
I begin.

I walk toward the morning sun,
glancing over my shoulder at the mound
    of snow
that is the soddy.
Soon,
it is impossible to say what is house
and what is prairie.

There's no creek to guide me.
Nothing is familiar,
but I push forward still.

Ma's dainty boots don't make walking easy,
but I am grateful for their cover.
Ice slips into the place I left unbuttoned,
and I tug one sock
and try to fasten a few buttons more.

There.
Just to my right,
paw prints in the snow.

He's still out here.
Was he separated from his pack?
Is he the weak one?
Has he eaten since the storm?

I secure the pillowcase
within the bodice of the red dress.
The quilt's folded over my coat,
wrapped from shoulders to elbows,
my threadbare armor.
I grip the broom handle in both hands,
ready.

The sun is higher now in the eastern sky.
A horse and a sleigh
have been through recently.
I'm unsure where these tracks came from
or where they lead,
but I can tell someone's traveled in two
    directions,
has doubled back.

I stay with the sleigh tracks
until they turn north,
away from home.

I could follow,
try to catch up,
but I won't.
I'm going home.
It's dangerous,
but it's what I've chosen,
and I gather strength from knowing this.

I lift each boot
just to plunge it deep into the snow again,
a high-step march that hardly travels forward.
The broom handle is my cane.
My forehead burns.
My chemise, drenched with sweat,
is a frigid layer against my skin.
And no matter how much snow I suck,
my stomach isn't tricked.

Wolf,
show your face.
This would be an easy fight
for you.

When the sun is behind me,
I rest for a bit.
The quilt is both my shawl and cushion.

Even though I've traveled since just after
   daybreak,
I feel no closer
to my home.
And I can't possibly know
exactly where home is.

The quilt is soaked through,
but I'm not yet ready to start again.
The western horizon, both blue and white,
is so bright it's hard to look at long.
The only tracks I see are my own.

I rock for warmth,
pulling the quilt about me like a hood.

What if this is the end?
What if I've fought my way from that prison
    for nothing,
just to die out here?

Tears freeze to my eyelashes
as I stumble to my feet,
which are weighty as sacks of flour.
My legs are wet
from stockings to bloomers.

My shadow extends long before me.
If I'm not home soon,
I will not last the night.

Finally I turn,
face the western sky,
and watch the sun sink
lower,
lower.
It is gone.
I must move while there's still light.
I stamp my feet to rouse them.
Pain shoots through my toes,
a promise I'm still living.

I trudge toward the purple darkness
and turn sometimes to see if the sunlight
has taken pity on me,
if it might wait to see me home.
But it is well beyond that imaginary place
where the sky meets land—
the only light just a memory of this day.

Do I see or hear it first,
the shadow where the sun
once was,
distant bells,
the unsure step of a horse's hooves
battling the snow?

Someone is there!
I'm certain now.
I try to run,
trip on Mrs. Oblinger's quilt,
crash to the ground,
but I am up again.

"Hello! Hello!"
My voice is firm, like I've used it every day.
I flap my arms,
and the quilt unfurls.

Now the sleigh bells ring clearly.
"Over here!" I say.
A sleigh is steering toward me.
The horse slows,
then stops.

"May Betterly?"

"I'm May," I say,
and reach forward.
A firm hand grasps my wrist.

"Miss Betterly," the stranger says,
"are you all right?"

I've seen nothing move
for so long,
save grass pushing at my feet,
clouds,
rabbits,
this endless blowing snow.
And this is a person!
He settles me in his sleigh,
pulls a buffalo robe around me.

In the moonlight,
I make out the man's blue muffler,
a hat pushed low on his brow.
His eyes;
I have seen them before.

"I'm John Chapman," he says.
"I helped Mr. Oblinger with his floor."

The neighbor who brought the wood.

If Ma could see me,
she'd tell me to remember my manners.

"How do you do, Mr. Chapman?"

He nods to me.
"How do you do?"

I'm riding in a sleigh
away from the Oblingers' soddy!

We pass a clump of darkness,
some trees I counted last July?

"The storm came the first of December,"
    he says.
"I dug out last week,
drove into town.
That's when I heard . . ."
His eyes dart to me.
". . . heard the Oblingers were gone.

Seemed funny Oblinger would leave
without telling me.
I'd helped him some at his place.
He'd done some work on mine.
I asked if anyone knew where he was headed.
Heard all sorts of stories,
none of them the same:
his wife had run,
he'd given up and sold his land,
he would come back with family next spring."

Desperate to find the missus,
how easy it would be
to forget me.

Mr. Chapman turns.

"No one mentioned a girl.
I got to thinking,
if he'd run off like some folks said,
and with those wolves about,
what had become of you?"

Someone has thought of me.
These last few days,
someone *knew*.

"I came earlier this week to look for you,"
Mr. Chapman says.

"A couple of miles from my place,
something along the creek caught my eye.
I dug through the snow,
reached the spokes of a wheel.
Oblinger's wagon must have overturned,
slid over the edge of the ravine."

My heart claws at my throat,
remembering the way Mr. Oblinger raced.
Something *had* happened to him.
Mr. Oblinger never made it to town?
"Did you see—?"

Mr. Chapman shakes his head.
"I walked around,
looked for more."
He clears his throat.

The wolves.
There is nothing I can say.

"Rode faster then,

when I figured you were alone,
but the snow blew through again.
It was a wonder I made it home.

I dug myself out this morning.
Tried again at the Oblingers' this afternoon.
When I reached the soddy,
I found a hole,
some footprints,
and the house empty.
Followed those prints
until I found you."

"It was good of you, Mr. Chapman."
"Nothing more than any decent person
    would do."

The horse labors in the snow;
still, we're moving faster
than I ever did alone.
I lay my head back against the robe's soft fur.
I will see my family soon.

"My folks are just a few miles
southeast of town," I say.

His eyes are soft.
"It was foolish of you to try
to make it on your own.
Foolish,
and brave."

"Guess I'm the foolish type, then."

He laughs,
but not unkindly.

It is strange to hear this story:
a man I'd barely met
taking the time
to try to save me.

I ask, "Could you tell me the day?"

"It's Friday,
the fifteenth of December."

Pa delivered me
to the Oblingers
five months ago.

I listen but don't talk much;
there is too much to consider.

I am content to feel the wind
at my cheeks,
to take in the stars
scattered like marbles across the heavens,
to watch the horse's sturdy legs
step gingerly.

"Pa said he'd come just before Christmas,"
I hear myself saying.

Mr. Chapman says,
"I must have just beat him."

The air is sharp in my lungs.
I'm dizzied
from hunger,
or a lack of sleep,
or from the sweet strangeness
of my circumstance.

If I had waited just a few hours more,
Mr. Chapman would have found me
still buried beneath the snow.

But I didn't wait;
I pulled myself out of that place
and set to walking.
I left a trail for Mr. Chapman
to come to me.

Even though the world has looked
much the same
since Mr. Chapman stopped for me,
I know we're getting nearer.
The land feels familiar,
and then I see the gentle rise,
a wisp of smoke
escaping from the chimney.

"Stop!"
I shout,
then remember myself.
"Please stop."

Pa dug out,
as I'd imagined.
The land between the house and barn is clear.
I race toward the door
and shove it open.
"Ma,
Pa,
Hiram!"
I call.

Ma steps forward.

"May?"
Her confusion breaking into a smile.
"What are you doing here?"
I hug her,
not yet ready to explain.

Over her shoulder I see Mr. Chapman
at the barn,
talking to Pa.

Hiram rushes from the barn.
"May Betts!"
he yells,
his face lighting with a grin.
"What happened to your hair?"

Suddenly we're all together
between the barn and soddy.
Pa folds me in his arms.
"You were alone?"
he whispers.

I nod,
soaking in the warmth of his overcoat.

Ma's brought a mug of coffee
and a square of corn bread,
thick,
delicious.
The coffee burns
as I gulp it down.

"She's a strong girl,"
Mr. Chapman says.

Hiram's eyes meet mine.

"A girl who tries to cover fifteen miles
alone in the snow can handle just about
    anything."

Pa clears his throat and squeezes me.
Ma wraps her arms around the both of us.
I close my eyes,
lean on Pa's shoulder.

In time,
I'll tell about the wolf,
the empty apple barrel,
and the darkness.
For now,
I need no words.

Later,
after Mr. Chapman has bid us
good night,
Hiram holds out his hand.
"Come with me," he says.
He leads me to the rise where in the spring,
the wildflowers grow.
We stand together, side by side.

I don't know why sometimes
reading works for me,
but other times it doesn't.

I don't know why holding something
helps my words to form.

Maybe I'll never understand
exactly why I struggle.
I am
smart and capable
(as Miss Sanders used to say).

But
tonight in this stillness,
I realize there's no shame in hoping

for things that might seem out of reach.
I will take the teaching examination
when I'm old enough,
and if I fail,
I'll try again.

"You can keep your Christmas candy.
I don't want it anymore."
Hiram's eyes grow wide.
"You've seen it?"
I smile.
"Not yet,
but just you wait."

Even though I know
my geography,
even though I understand what is and
    isn't real,
there's no reason to stop hoping
that sometime
I might find it,
that distant place
where the sun journeys
and earth at last meets sky.

# A Note from the Author

Growing up, I fell in love with the Little House books and talked about Laura Ingalls Wilder as if she were someone I knew personally. In the late nineteenth century, when Laura was a girl, schoolwork focused on recitation and memorization and favored students able to do those things well. When I became a teacher, I grew curious about what life must have been like for frontier children who found schooling a challenge. Would a girl who couldn't read well have been kept out of school? Would she have been chastised for not trying hard enough? Or would her intelligence have been recognized?

In this book, May struggles with dyslexia, a learning disability that hampers a person's capacity to process what is read. Dyslexia was unknown in the nineteenth century. It varies in each reader, although difficulties with reading fluency, word recognition, and comprehension are common, as are the omission of words and anxiety stemming from reading aloud. The techniques that prove helpful to May (repetition, reading in unison with one or more people, holding objects) have benefited many with dyslexia.

While *May B.* is a work of fiction, I've used the short-grass prairie of western Kansas as inspiration, imagining the Betterlys' and Oblingers' soddies in the outlying areas of Gove County. In the late 1870s, this part of Kansas was sparsely settled. Families homesteaded far from established towns, with neighbors miles away.

School terms typically ran summer and winter, allowing children to work during planting and harvest. Teachers were often young single women, as it was possible to receive a teaching certificate at fifteen or sixteen.

The text quoted in this book is from *The American Educational*

*Reader, Number 5* (Ivison, Blakeman, Taylor, & Co., 1873), which I found in an antique shop just as I was starting to work on *May B*. I don't know if this book would have been available in Kansas schoolhouses at this time, though a similar reader would have been. Children often worked with the books accessible to them, many using in school the texts their families had brought from other parts of the country. I've included three lessons: "The Grandeur of the Sea" (author unknown), "A Hasty and Unjust Judgment," the passage about Mr. Goodman (attributed to "Aiken, adapted"), and "The Voice of the Wind" (author unknown). The last stanza of the poem is my own invention, something I altered to create more dramatic movement within the story.

For those interested in learning more about Kansas history, frontier living, or dyslexia, here are some helpful resources:

The Kansas Historical Society: kshs.org

The Prairie Museum of Art and History (Colby, Kansas): prairiemuseum.org

The International Dyslexia Association: interdys.org

# Acknowledgments

Many thanks to those who have played a role in the creation of this book:

It's not often an author is lucky enough to write for two different editors. Nicole Geiger has been an unflagging enthusiast, careful reader, and mentor through this whole process. When she told me *May B.* was the sort of book she'd loved as a child, I knew it would be safe in her hands. Emily Seife's commitment to May and her personal growth pushed me to discover new ways to challenge my character and flesh her out more fully. Emily, I've appreciated every honest "not there yet" that has kept me working hard.

Michelle Humphrey, my agent, who found me in the slush and took a chance on my quiet verse novel. Your positive attitude and commitment as a colleague and friend have been invaluable.

Chris Griffin, of the Prairie Museum of Art and History in Colby, Kansas, for answering my questions about the landscape, plants, animals, insects, and waterways of western Kansas and for recommending reader and Kansas expert Ann Miner. Any inaccuracies that remain in the story are mine alone.

Shawn Goodman, fellow Elevensie author and literacy expert, for your insight into the frustrations and insecurities a dyslexic child experiences, as well as for sharing common reading challenges.

Ellen Ruffin and Abbie Woolridge of the de Grummond Children's Literature Collection and author Kate Bernheimer for answering my questions about Hansel and Gretel.

My parents, Milt and Polly, who made books a natural part of my upbringing; my grandparents, Dick and Gene, for exposing me to authors from Beatrix Potter to Wallace Stegner and for encouraging my imagination; and my sister, Chris, one of my biggest cheerleaders.

Dayle Arceneaux and Bonnie Rehage of the Bayou Readers' and Authors' Guild for encouraging me to continue this experiment in verse. My online critique partners, Denise Jaden, Weronika Janczuk, Elle Strauss, and Natalie Bahm, for your keen eyes. Natalie, I will be forever grateful for your question that led me to a newer, stronger ending.

Jamie Martin, for pointing me toward your antiques-shop find, the reader that played such a large part in the creation of this story, and for believing that this story had to be shared.

Molly Bolton and the rest of the Jambalaya Writers' Conference coordinators, for seeing promise in my story.

Dr. Jack Bedell of Southeastern Louisiana University, for including several early poems in *Louisiana Literature* magazine.

Cheryl Matherne, principal of St. Matthew's Episcopal School in Houma, Louisiana, for the beautiful way you supported my decision to devote myself to writing full-time, and for your love for this character.

C. S. Neal, for capturing perfectly with your artwork the atmosphere of the book. Your cover reminds me of beloved stories from my own childhood.

For the women who have gone before me: As Kansas historian Lilla Day Monroe said, "The world has never seen such hardihood, such perseverance, such devotion, nor such ingenuity in making the best of everything as was displayed by America's pioneer women. Their like has never been known" (Joanna Stratton, *Pioneer Women: Voices from the Kansas Frontier*, Touchstone, 1982, page 21).

My husband, Dan, and my boys, Noah and Caleb: it isn't easy living with someone who for years chases an impossible dream. Thank you for giving me the room and time to make a try at being a writer. And always, thank you for your love. You three mean the world to me.

And finally, my deepest gratitude to the One who binds up the brokenhearted and who extends dignity and compassion to the forgotten.

# About the Author

Caroline Starr Rose spent her childhood in the deserts of Saudi Arabia and New Mexico, camping at the Red Sea in one and eating red chile in the other. As a girl she danced ballet, raced through books by Laura Ingalls Wilder, and put on magic shows in a homemade cape. She has taught social studies and English, and worked to instill in her students a passion for books, an enthusiasm for experimenting with words, and a curiosity about the past. She lives in New Mexico. Visit her at carolinestarrrose.com.